GEORGIA O'KEEFFE

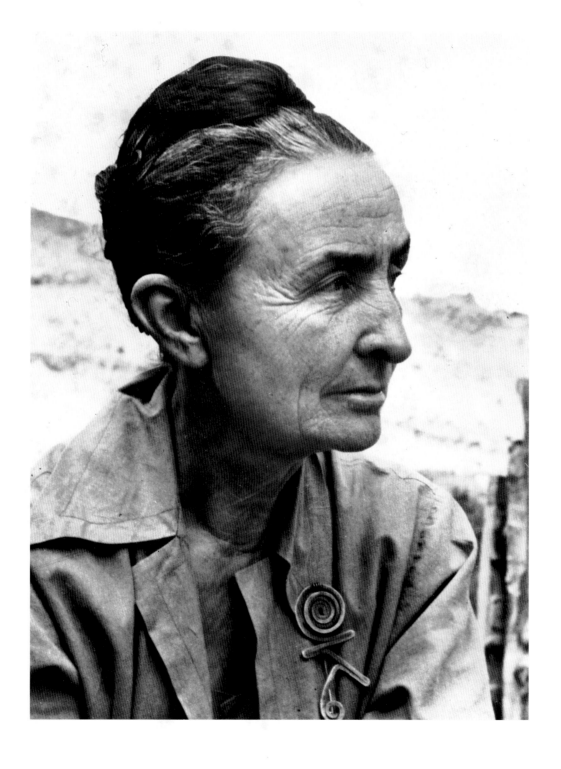

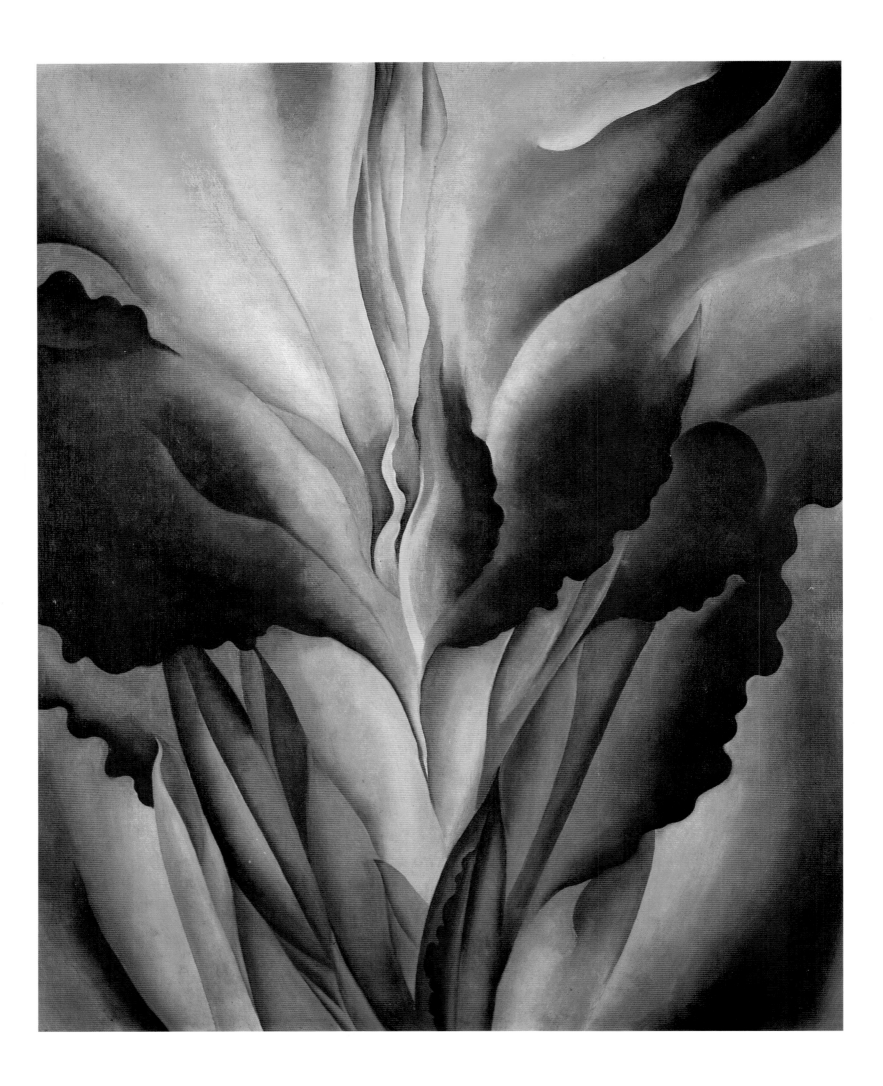

GEORGIA O'KEEFFE

Nancy Frazier

JG PRESS

Reprinted 2004 by
World Publications Group, Inc
455 Somerset Avenue
North Dighton, MA 02764

ISBN 1-57215-300-8

Printed in China

ACKNOWLEDGMENTS
The publisher would like to thank the following people who have helped
in the preparation of this book: Rita Longabucco, who did the picture
research; Barbara Thrasher, who edited it; and Don Longabucco, who
designed it.

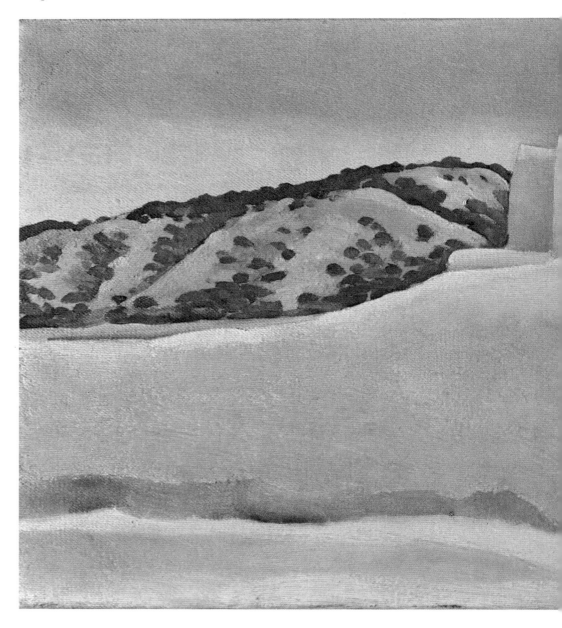

Page 2:
Red Canna
c. 1924, oil on canvas mounted on masonite,
36×29⅞ in.
Gift of Oliver James,
University of Arizona Museum of Art, Tucson, AZ

This page:
Another Church, Hernandez, New Mexico
1931, oil on canvas, 10×24 in.
Courtesy of The Anschutz Collection

Contents

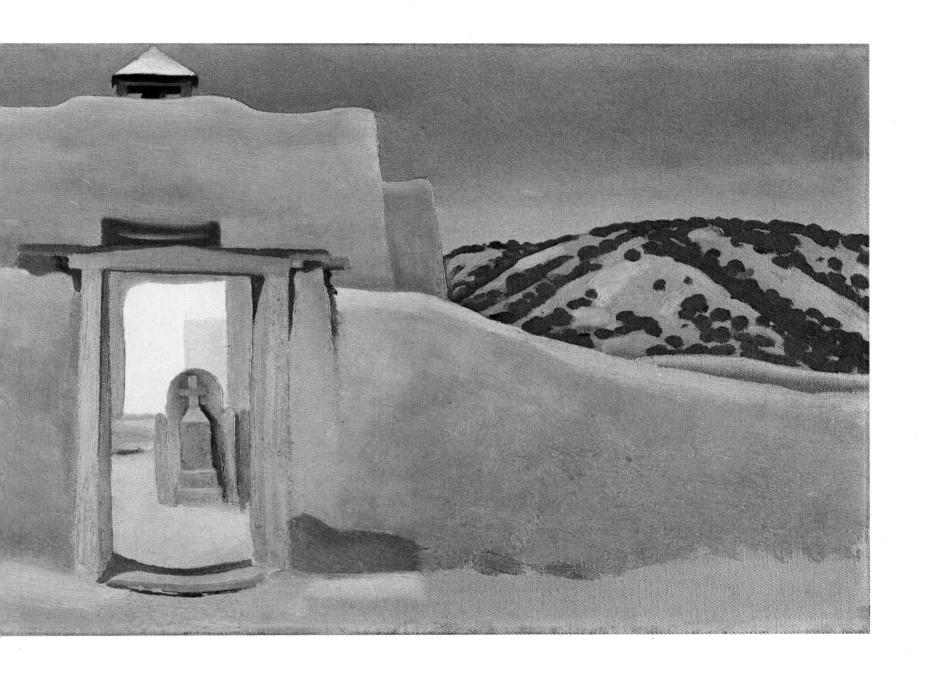

INTRODUCTION

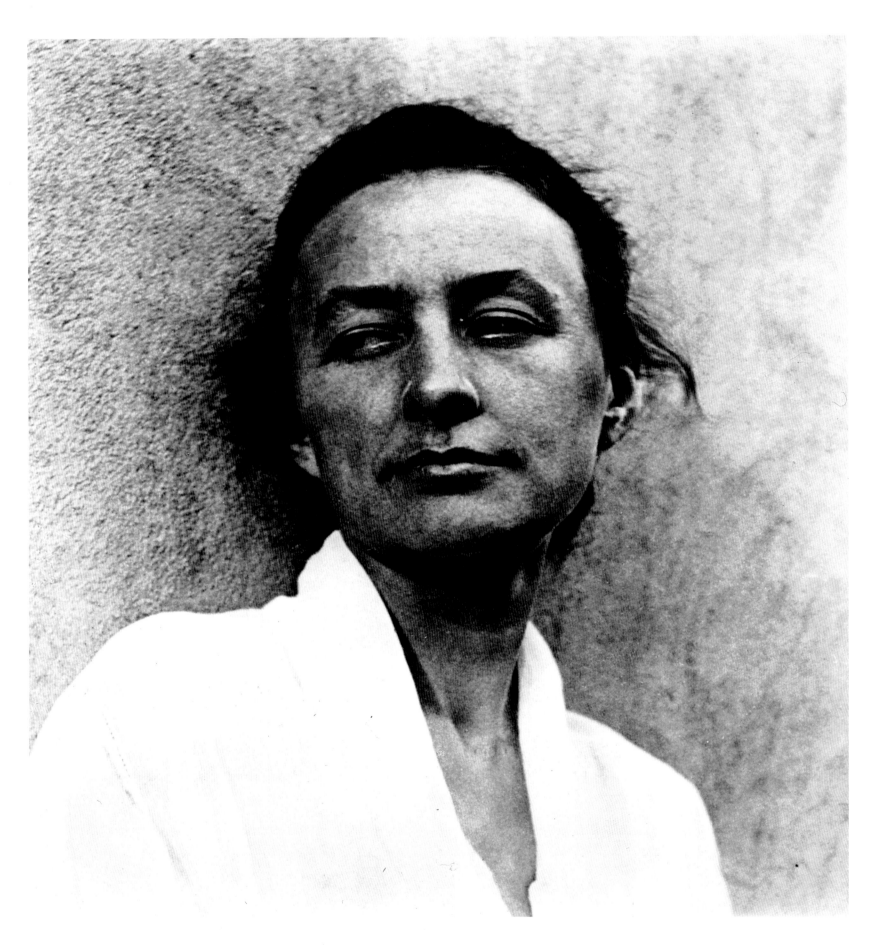

Georgia O'Keeffe was a myth in her own lifetime. She was a beautiful young woman who became more handsome as she aged. She had fine bones, a perfect mouth, serious grayish-green eyes and an aloof aura. Photographs of Georgia O'Keeffe led one to expect a tall woman with a strong voice, since she held herself aristocratically straight with an air of authority. Yet in person she was smaller than expected, and she spoke softly, although firmly. She painted with brilliant, dazzling colors, but year in, year out, she wore a simple white or black dress. She seemed remote, and during the last 40 years of her life she seemed to live a reclusive, ascetic life in the New Mexico desert, although she was far more sociable than outsiders realized.

Georgia O'Keeffe died in 1986 at the age of 98. She had been in the front ranks among her contemporaries of both sexes – breaking convention and setting direction without reference to gender – for decades. Although she continues to fall in and out of favor among art critics, she was a supremely talented artist with unique vision. Lewis Mumford, a critic of wide repute, wrote about her in 1927, "Miss O'Keeffe is perhaps the most original painter in America." She was one of the artists in a 1958 exhibition presented by the Metropolitan Museum of Art called "Fourteen American Masters, Paintings from Colonial Times to the Present." In the catalogue her work was evaluated

and assessed: "There is no doubt that the purity of her style has had considerable influence on applied design and even the architecture of our day. Georgia O'Keeffe has been said to be our greatest living woman painter."

That Georgia O'Keeffe is controversial is one good reason to take her work seriously. Another is that she is one of the few artists in history who have changed the way we look at things. It is difficult to see the skull of a large animal without thinking of O'Keeffe's extraordinary paintings of dry, sun- and desert-bleached skulls. Her startling, close-up, magnified flower paintings forever affect the way we look at flowers. And Vincent Van Gogh may have co-opted the sunflower (although O'Keeffe painted a formidable one), but ever since that 1987 show for which an enormous brilliant red poppy was used as

Left: This photographic portrait of Georgia O'Keeffe was taken by Paul Strand in 1930, when O'Keeffe was 43 years old.

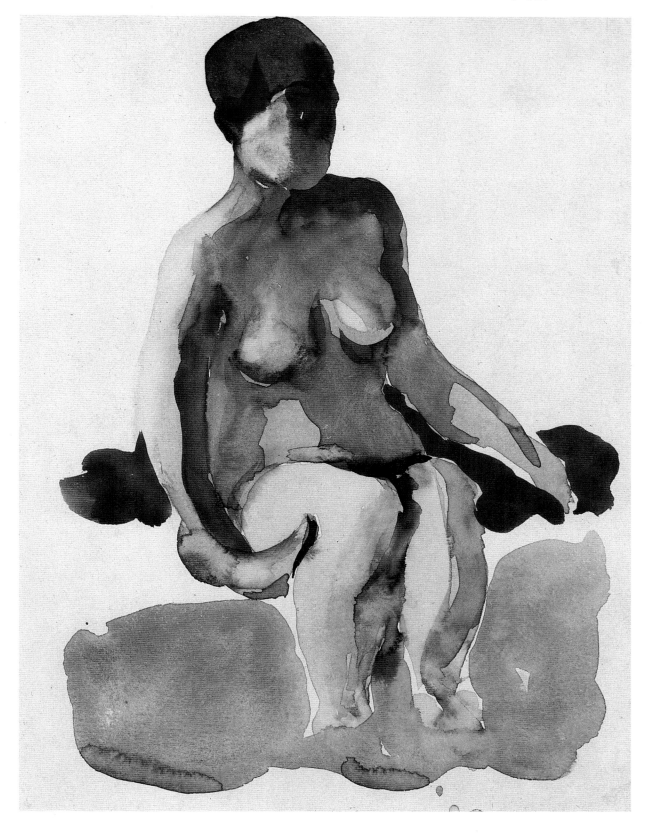

Right: Georgia O'Keeffe painted *Seated Nude X* in watercolor in 1917. She painted few nudes in her lifetime, and the ones she did are female bodies. (The Metropolitan Museum of Art, New York, N.Y.)

advertisement, O'Keeffe and the poppy are synonymous. As to the folding purple, red, tan and black hills of New Mexico, O'Keeffe's paintings of the landscape near her home in Abiquiu are mental previews for any traveler in the Southwest. They also have a spiritual power, if not dogma. One can not help but wonder about the history of this woman who painted such interesting pictures.

Sun Prairie, Wisconsin, had a population of well under a thousand people when Georgia O'Keeffe was born there on November 15, 1887. She was the second child, first daughter, of Ida and Francis O'Keeffe, and the birth, attended by a country doctor, was in their own farmhouse. Francis O'Keeffe was a diligent and prosperous farmer who worked 600 acres when his first children were born. Cattle and horses, geese,

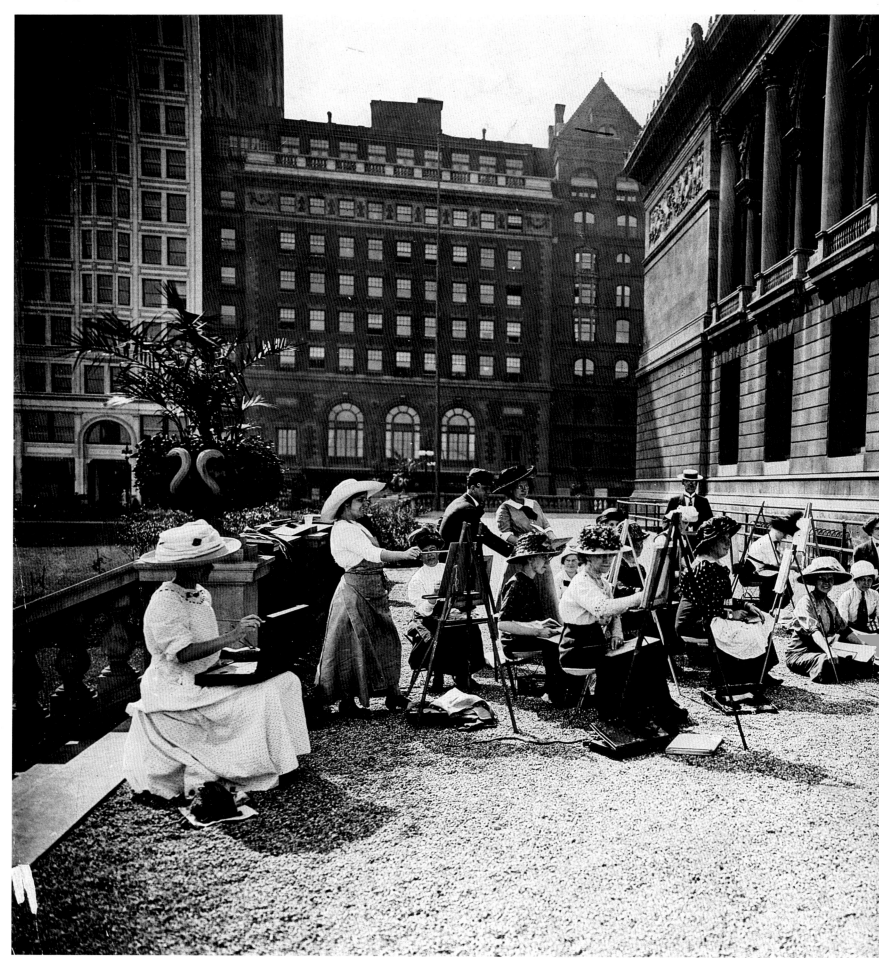

apple trees, corn fields, wagonloads of hay, fields of wildflowers and, as the name of the place implies, plenty of sky and sunshine above wide flat plain – these were some of Georgia O'Keeffe's earliest memories. "Papa had a prize farm," she once told a friend. "There was no better one in Sun Prairie. Although he had plenty of farm help, he worked from dawn to dark."

Francis O'Keeffe's parents had immigrated to America from Ireland after their wool business failed. They had begun buying land and homesteading in 1848. Ida Totto, who would become Francis's wife, lived nearby the O'Keeffe farm. Her father had served in an unsuccessful Hungarian effort to overthrow Austrian rule and was a political refugee in America. Ida's Dutch ancestors on her mother's side went all the way back to New Amsterdam of 1637. So the Totto side of the family had an exotic flair compared to the down-to-earth O'Keeffes.

There was as much difference in the personalities of her mother and father as there was in their parentage. Francis, Georgia's father, was remembered by his daughter as a cheerful,

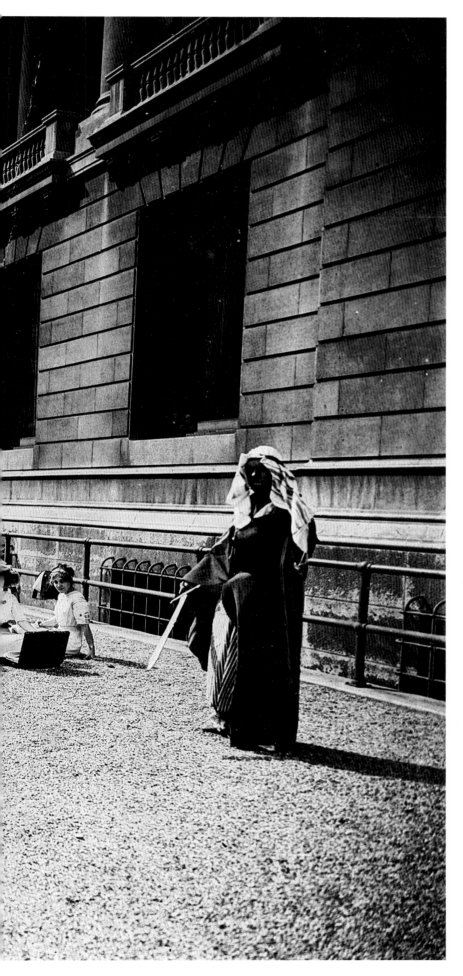

Left: An outdoor sketch class at the Art Institute of Chicago in 1918, 12 years after O'Keeffe studied there.

Below: William Merritt Chase poses with one of the fish paintings for which he became well-known. O'Keeffe studied with Chase at New York's Art Students League.

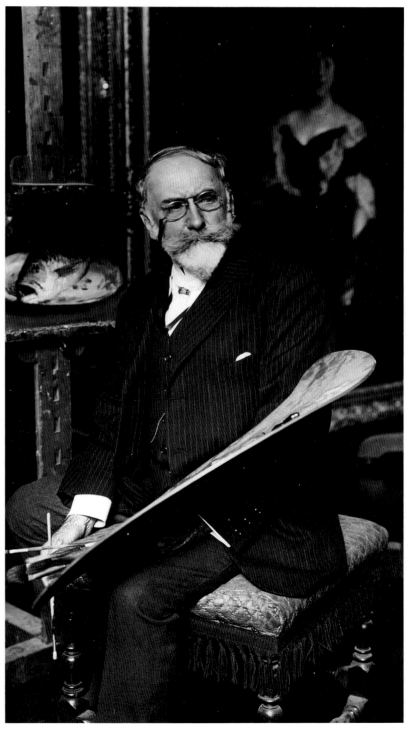

warm-hearted, fun-loving, handsome man. Her mother was the opposite. She was intellectually inclined, demanding, undemonstrative, and intent upon her children – seven in number altogether – getting a good education. She often read to them, and Georgia would always remember those hours fondly, especially the stories about pioneer life and adventures that whetted her appetite to see America's West.

As part of her daughters' education, Ida O'Keeffe first gave them books from which to study drawing. Then, when Georgia was nearly 12, her mother arranged painting lessons for them. These they took in town, some three and a half miles by horse and buggy, every Saturday. Georgia very soon knew that she'd found her calling and told a friend, with no uncertainty, that she planned to be an artist when she grew up.

The first 14 years of her life were spent in comfort and security among a large, stable family in a midwestern setting for which she felt deep affection. At 14 she was sent away to a convent boarding school near Madison, Wisconsin, while her family prepared to move to Williamsburg, Virginia, and the next year she went to the Madison high school. Prompted by the death of his three brothers who contracted tuberculosis, in addition to the harsh winters and rigors of farming, Francis O'Keeffe had decided to sell the farm and move to a kinder climate. Ida was highly agreeable to this decision, pleased with the opportunity to settle in the small but cultured town of Williamsburg, home of the College of William and Mary. They bought a large, white clapboard house that looked quite similar to their Sun Prairie farmhouse. Georgia was sent to the Chatham Episcopal Institute in Chatham, Virginia, 200 miles from home.

By the time she had reached Chatham, Georgia O'Keeffe was independent enough to be eccentric. Besides being the only Northerner in this decidedly Southern academy, she dressed as she pleased, in simple, austere, loose-fitting dresses rather than the ruffled feminine clothes of the times. She also wore her hair pulled back in the stern fashion that she never changed. Later she would remember that period as important especially because of her long walks in the hills "with the line of the Blue Ridge Mountains on the horizon calling me, as distances have always called me." Yet she was not unfriendly or antisocial. To the contrary she was a sorority sister (Kappa Delta), on the basketball team, in the German club, and treasurer of the tennis club. She joined in pranks with high spirits while keeping her reputation as a nonconformist.

"I only remember two things I painted in those years," she wrote many years later, "a large bunch of purple lilacs and some red and yellow corn – both painted with the wet-paper method on full-sized sheets of rough Whatman paper. . . . I remember wondering how I could paint the big shapes of bunches of lilacs and – at the same time – each little flower. I slapped my paint about quite a bit and didn't care where it spilled."

Of tremendous importance during this time was the admira-

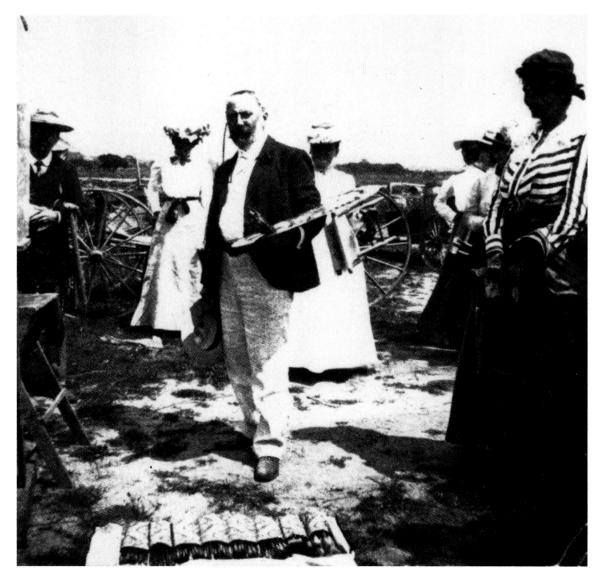

Left: William Merritt Chase with students at Shinnecock Hills, c. 1901. Although Chase taught painting in his own nineteenth-century style, O'Keeffe gained a great deal from his still life class. For her *Rabbit and Copper Pot* (1907), which has been likened to Chase's *English Cod* (1904), O'Keeffe won the Chase Scholarship and a chance for further study.

Right: Marcel Duchamp's *Nude Descending a Staircase* fueled controversy at the 1913 Armory Show in New York. The show stirred interest in "modern" art, creating an exciting atmosphere for O'Keeffe and other artists. (Philadelphia Museum of Art, PA)

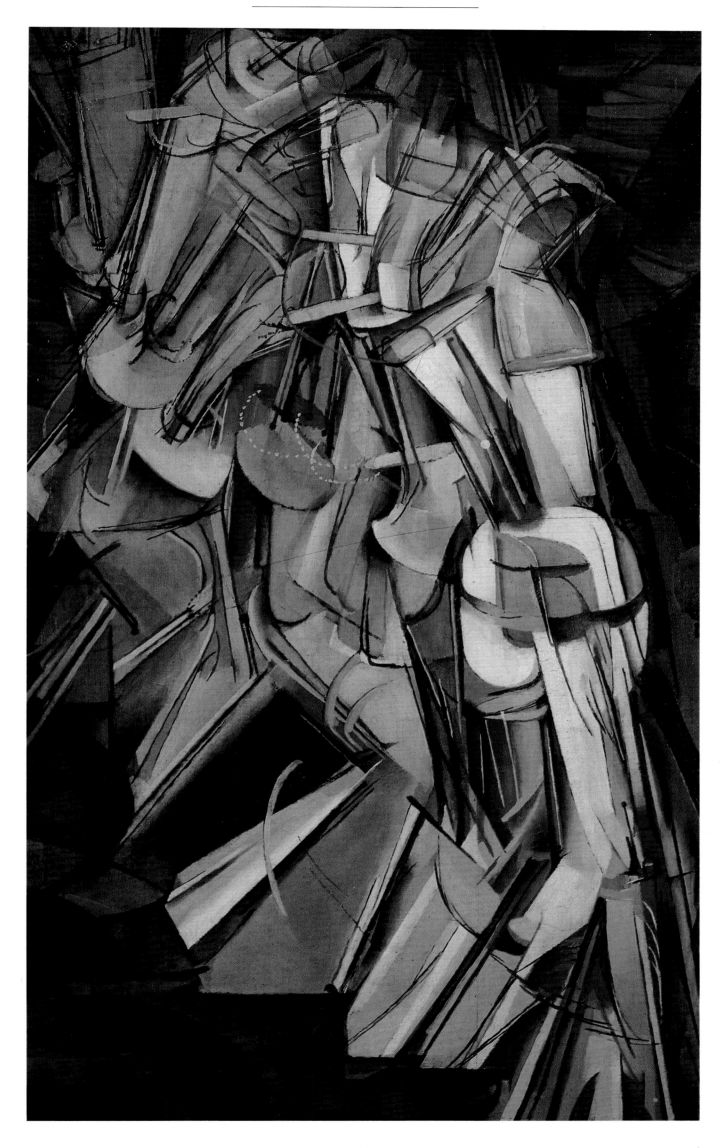

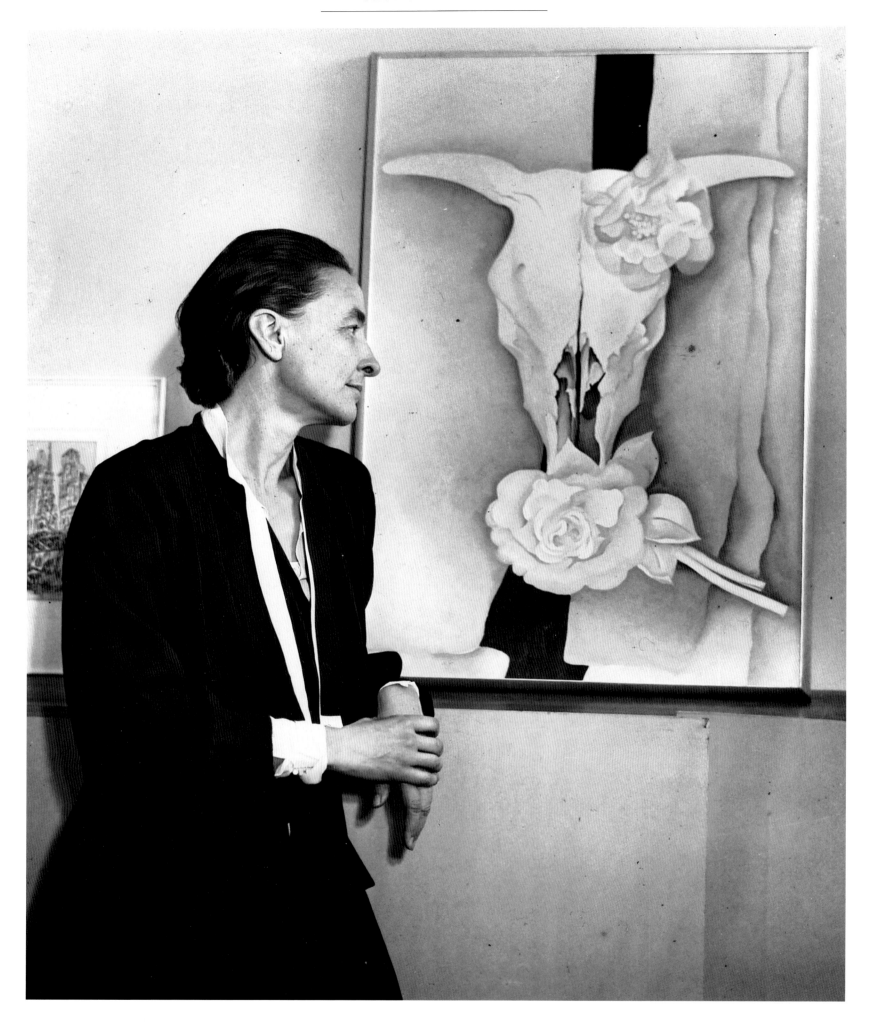

tion and encouragement Georgia received from the principal at Chatham, Elizabeth May Willis, who was also the art teacher. She saw Georgia's talent and encouraged it unstintingly. Even in later years Willis followed O'Keeffe's career, inviting her to substitute as art teacher when she herself took a few months off,

and traveling to New York to see exhibits of her student's work many years later.

In Williamsburg, the grocery business Francis had tried did not succeed, nor did his other efforts to establish himself in business. While Georgia, who graduated from Chatham at the

12

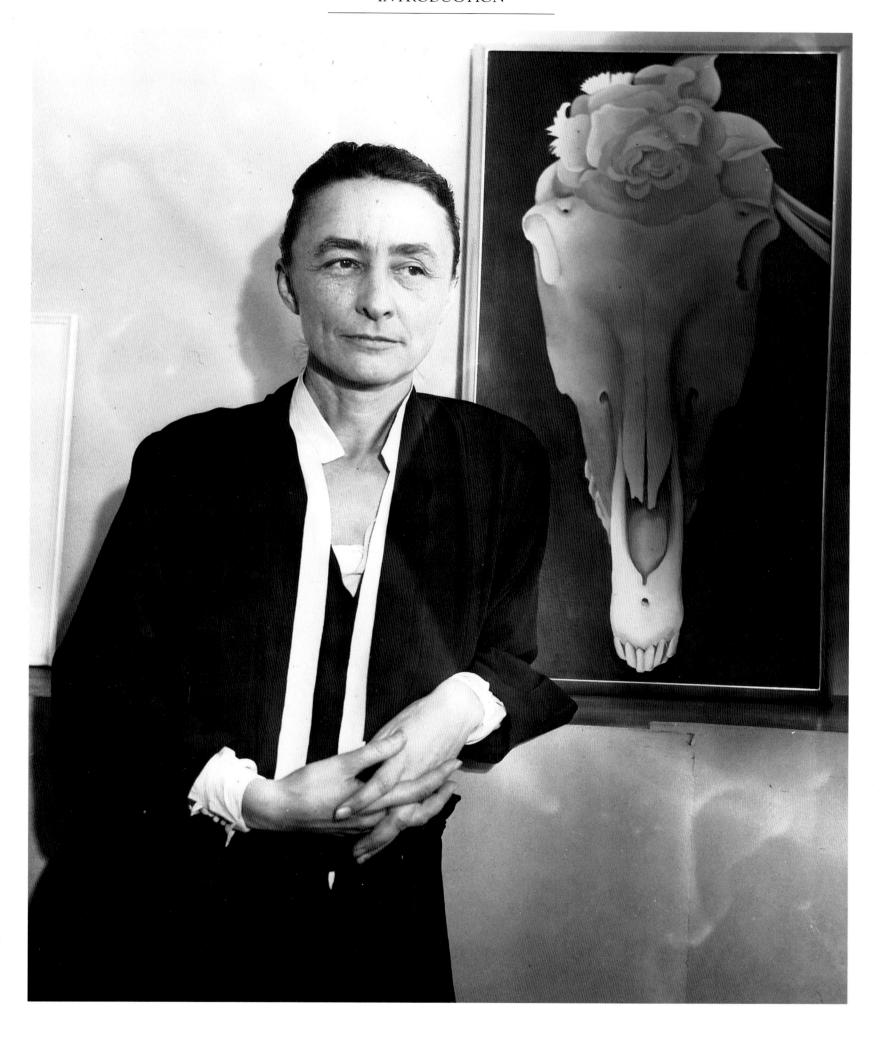

Opposite: The artist poses at an exhibition at An American Place with her painting, *Cow's Skull with Calico Roses*, December 29, 1931.

Above: O'Keeffe with *Horse's Skull with White Rose* at the 1931 exhibition at Alfred Stieglitz's An American Place.

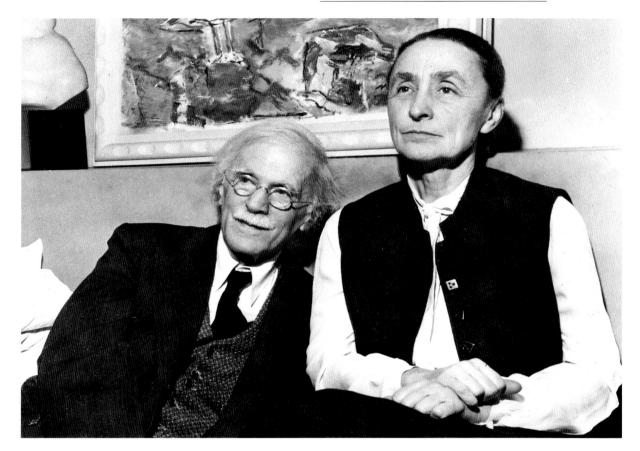

Left: Even after Alfred Stieglitz and Georgia O'Keeffe were married in 1924 – she was 24 years his junior – they maintained autonomy, sometimes living apart.

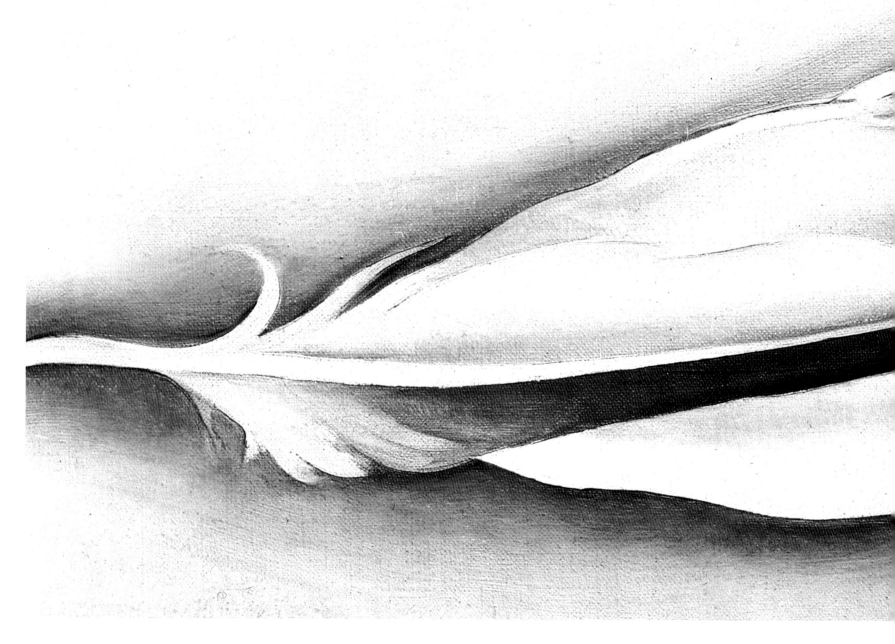

age of 17, went on to study at the Art Institute of Chicago (living with relatives on her mother's side of the family), the family fortune was in decline, and by 1907 Mrs. O'Keeffe was taking in boarders.

"I have never understood why we had such dark olive green rooms for art schools," O'Keeffe would eventually comment about the Chicago Institute. The year she spent there was strange and full of surprises, mostly unpleasant. She was, as she later wrote, "a little girl with a big black ribbon bow on my braid of hair." As she sat there in one of those dark rooms at the beginning of her anatomy course, to her mortification out walked a completely naked man. She burned with embarrassment and never remembered anything about that class. "It was a suffering. The class only came once a week and I had to make up my mind what I was going to do about it before time for the next lesson. I still had the idea that I wanted to be an artist. I thought that meant I had to go to art school. Drawing casts in the upstairs gallery wouldn't go on forever. . . . I don't remember learning anything except that I finally became accustomed to the idea of the nude model."

If she became more accustomed to nude models, she did not become more interested in them. In her life's work, there are almost no studies of the human form, and the few nudes she did are female bodies. She did, however, benefit from John Vanderpoel's lectures on drawing the human figure at the Institute and he, in turn, judged her work favorably. Undaunted in her pursuit of art, she planned to go on to New York City and the Art Students League, which her former mentor, Elizabeth May Willis, had attended. But that next step was delayed a year because, upon returning home to Williamsburg, she came down with typhoid fever.

It was a long intermission between classes but in September, 1907, Georgia O'Keeffe took the train trip to New York City. Her year at the Art Students League seems to have held large measures of frustration and confusion as well as reward. She loved the still life class with William Merritt Chase, one of the foremost painters of the day, whose feet were, however, solidly planted in the nineteenth century. His best-known paintings are light-filled studies of women, idealized femininity, but in England he gained a reputation as a painter of fish! Seriously so: the elegance of his rendering of shimmering sequin-like scales earned him accolades. The similarity between Chase's *English*

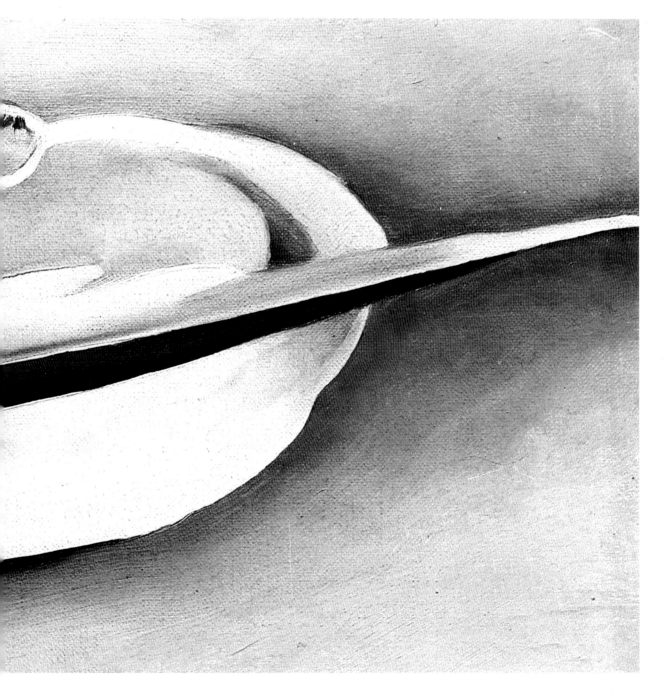

Left: Georgia O'Keeffe's oil painting, *Shell and Feather* measures 6-by-12-inches. (Colby College Art Museum, Waterville, ME).

Cod (1904) and Georgia O'Keeffe's *Rabbit and Copper Pot* (1907) has much to do with the setting, objects provided by Chase no doubt. "I loved the colors of the brass and copper pots and pans," O'Keeffe once wrote. Her success with the rabbit and pot won her the Chase Scholarship, which brought with it an opportunity to take courses at the League's Lake George summer school, in upstate New York.

Two curiously premonitory events occurred during that year in New York. For one, another student, Eugene Speicher, persuaded O'Keeffe to pose for him rather than go to the class to which she was on her way. One of his comments was, "It doesn't matter what you do, I'm going to be a great painter and you will probably end up teaching painting in some girls' school." Though he did become a respected painter who had many shows and won many awards, and though she did spend time teaching at a girls' school, ironically enough the painting chosen to represent Speicher during the League's 100th anniversary show was the portrait he painted that school year, 1908, of Georgia O'Keeffe. More ironic still, as famous as he became, she became more so. Poetic justice, perhaps.

Also during 1908, O'Keeffe, Speicher and a group of their classmates visited 291, the abbreviated name for The Little Galleries of the Photo-Secession at 291 Fifth Avenue that photographer Alfred Stieglitz opened in New York City, and in which he was showing outrageous new art – Rodin at that time. Stieglitz was one of the most influential supporters of unconventional artistic talent in the United States. But 1908 was early in the annals of modern art, and the students went to 291 to argue with Stieglitz, not support him. The conversation became so unpleasantly hostile that O'Keeffe retreated into another room. Although the Rodin drawings didn't impress her greatly just then – they were just a lot of scribbles as far as she was concerned – they had a delayed effect. The few nudes she painted, in later years, bear strong resemblance to those of Rodin as well as works of Matisse and Picasso that, in time, she also saw at 291.

After her summer at Lake George, O'Keeffe did not resume her studies at the League. Probably because the family finances were in poor condition, she returned to live with her Chicago relatives and found work as a commercial artist, drawing lace and embroidery for advertisements for a couple of years. A case of measles left her eyes temporarily weakened and she returned to Virginia. It was a gloomy period for Georgia O'Keeffe: her mother had contracted the tuberculosis her father so much feared and her health was very frail, her father was unable to

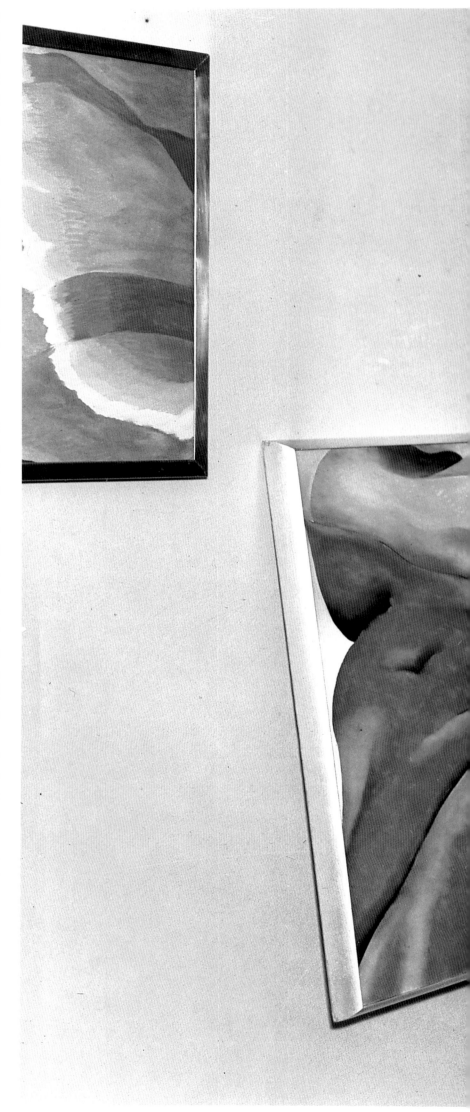

Right: Alfred Stieglitz poses with O'Keeffe's paintings after giving a lecture to New York School of Industrial Art students, December 2, 1936.

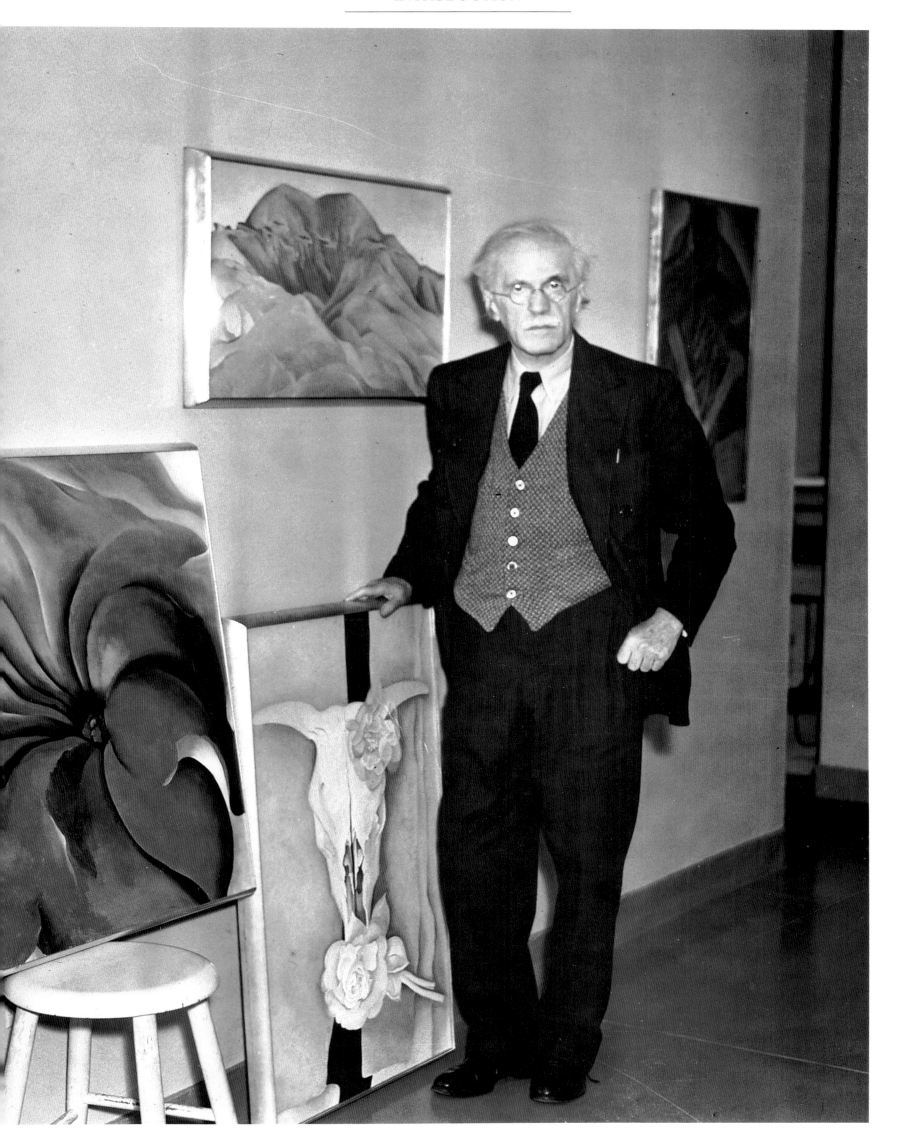

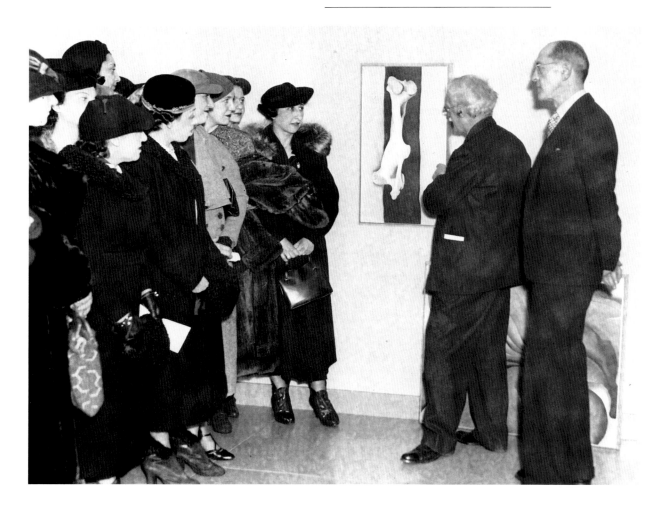

succeed in business, and her parents' marriage was an unhappy one. Georgia herself seemingly abandoned her dream of becoming a painter.

Then, in the summer of 1912 she took a course at the University of Virginia in Charlottesville and it marked a new direction for her career. In the first place she studied with Aloon Bement, an apostle for the inspiring ideas of Arthur Wesley Dow, head of the fine arts department at Teachers College of Columbia University. Dow's innovations, which Georgia found provocative and liberating, moved away from the tradition of copying nature and provided exercises that led toward the principles of abstraction. This allowed for individual expression and mandated only filling the spaces on a page beautifully. Dow devised exercises that used lines and stressed rhythm, subordination and balance. These were concepts that resonated in harmony with O'Keeffe's drive to create art that was personal and expressive of her own feelings. Other more mundane opportunities also began to fall into place. With Bement's help and then with a connection made for her by a Chatham school friend from Texas, she secured academic posts both in Amarillo, Texas, for the school year and at the University of Virginia, working with Bement, during the summer.

Texas suited her. "That was my country," she said of the Amarillo plains where she spent two years, "terrible winds and a wonderful emptiness." The land, she said, was like the ocean all around you. "Hardly anybody liked it, but I loved it." And during the summer, in Charlottesville where her family now lived, she taught drawing. It was as though, after an intermission, her artistic identity began to mature and seek self definition. She returned to New York in the fall of 1914 to study with

Arthur Dow at Columbia. It was the year following an historic art event, the 1913 Armory Show in New York in which "modern" art, such as had only been seen at Stieglitz's small 291 gallery before, was shown to the American public at large. The Armory exhibition had works by Rodin, Picasso, Bracque and Matisse as well as many of the American artists whom Stieglitz championed. It became recognized as a turning point – art shunned by the museums was gaining public recognition and fueling controversy. Marcel Duchamp's *Nude Descending a Staircase* was the most talked about and ridiculed piece in the exhibit.

Georgia O'Keeffe had missed seeing the Armory Show, but she strode unhaltingly into the atmosphere of excitement that followed in its wake. She visited 291 from time to time. And she met Anita Pollitzer, a fellow student whose friendship endured after O'Keeffe left New York to teach again at the University of Virginia during the summer and then, successively in Columbia, South Carolina and Canyon, Texas. Through correspondence and publications she kept up with the latest exhibitions and gossip about art. With Anita Pollitzer she exchanged not just letters but also ideas, dreams and drawings. "Anita? What is art – anyway? When I think of how hopelessly unable I am to answer that question I cannot help feeling like a farce – pretending to teach anybody anything about it," she wrote in October, 1915. In her memoir, *A Woman On Paper*, which includes letters the two exchanged, Anita Pollitzer wrote, "One day after Christmas in 1915, Georgia sent me a roll of drawings with the express injunction that I was to show them to no one. . . . I was struck by their livingness. Here were sensitive charcoals, on the same kind of paper that all art students were using, and through no trick, no superiority of tools, they were expressing what I felt had not been said in any art I had seen; and what they were expressing seemed important and beautiful." Pollitzer had been discovering contemporary art at Stieglitz's 291 and, as she wrote, "At certain moments in our lives we know what we must do, and when I saw Georgia's drawings, it was such a moment."

It was a dreary, rainy day and Stieglitz was in a mood that matched the weather until Anita Pollitzer, without speaking about the artist, spread the work O'Keeffe had sent her on the floor in front of him. It was then Stieglitz made his famous comment, "Finally a woman on paper!" Women had, of course, been on paper, canvas and most other media, and marvelously so, long before Stieglitz "discovered" O'Keeffe. Still, since

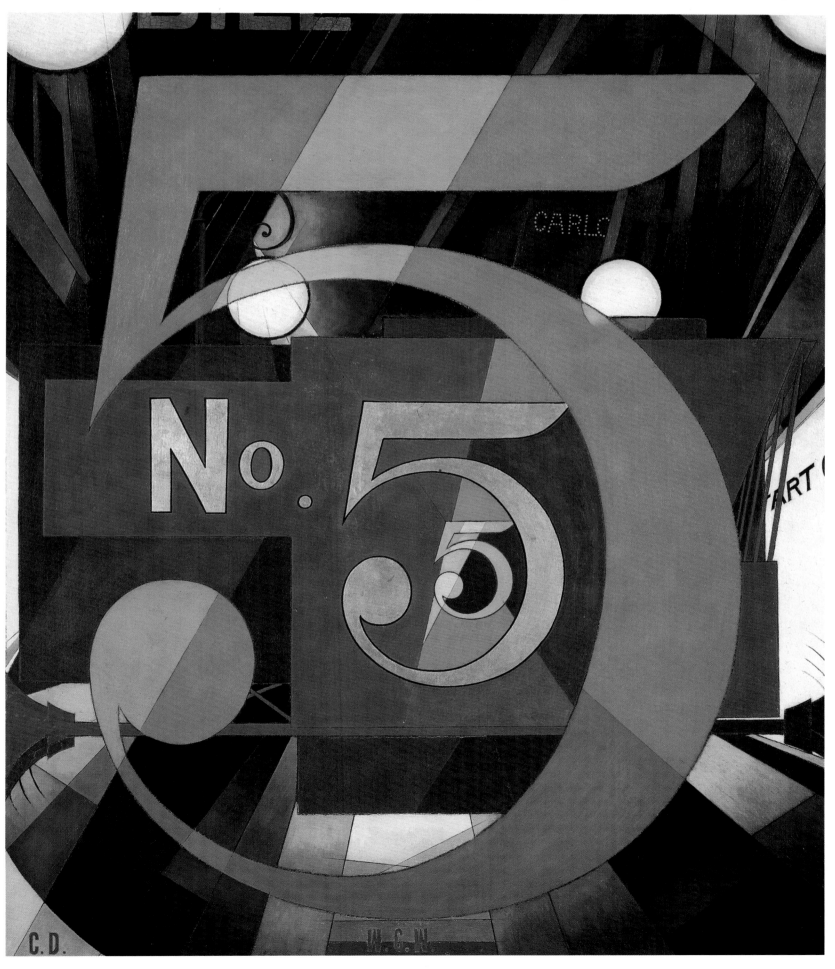

Stieglitz had been finding and championing artists for several years, his pleasure in seeing the work of an obviously talented unknown woman must have been immense.

The message from Stieglitz that Pollitzer conveyed to O'Keeffe, in breaking the news that she had shown him the drawings, was, "Tell her they're the purest, fairest, sincerest things that have entered 291 in a long while." He mentioned showing them in the gallery. To be appreciated by the impresario of the current art scene was sublime – both exhilarating and terrible. In the mix was the fear the bubble would burst, the distress at having her strongly emotional, personal work seen by strangers, the heady pleasure of recognition and an odd sense of confusion, perhaps insecurity, about what Stieglitz found appealing in her work. She wrote to him and asked.

"My dear Miss O'Keeffe," he wrote back. "What am I to say? It is impossible for me to put into words what I saw and felt in your drawings. As a matter of fact I would not make any attempt to do so. I might give you what I received from them if you and I were to meet and talk about life." Before they did meet, O'Keeffe returned to New York to take a summer teaching methods course – a prerequisite for a post she'd been offered at a college in Canyon, Texas – and discovered that, without her knowledge, Stieglitz had, indeed, hung her drawings at 291. She found out about it accidentally from another student who had seen a bulletin board notice about the exhibition. "I was startled and shocked. For me the drawings were private and the idea of their being hung on the wall for the public to look at was just too much. I went immediately to 291 and asked Stieglitz to take the drawings down," O'Keeffe recorded many years later. "He said he wanted them on the wall to look at. . . . Stieglitz and I argued and though I didn't like it, I went away leaving the drawings on the wall."

That year, 1916, was like a threshold to the rest of her life. Besides her work achieving recognition by being shown at 291 – on two occasions – it was the year she and Stieglitz began to mean so much to one another, and the year when she went to Canyon, Texas, as head of the art department at West Texas State Normal College. It is also the year her mother died.

From 1916 until Stieglitz died in 1946, his and Georgia O'Keeffe's life were intertwined. He was 24 years older than she (a few months older than her mother, in fact), and married. He provided her the financial opportunity to stop teaching and devote herself to painting. They began living together in 1918. Stieglitz and his wife divorced, and he and O'Keeffe were married in December, 1924 – a step she was reluctant to take but he insisted upon. She was then 37 and he nearly 61. They did not exchange rings, nor did she agree to the traditional vows to "love, honor, and obey," and she insisted upon keeping her own name – at least half a century before any of this became widely acceptable.

In his role as finder and promoter of artists, Stieglitz was particularly supportive of a small circle that, besides O'Keeffe, was made up of photographer Paul Strand and painters John Marin, Arthur Dove, Charles Demuth and Marsden Hartley. All were influenced by the abstract art movement and each influenced the other, sometimes in obvious ways, sometimes more subtly. Although Stieglitz closed 291 in 1917, he was able to show "his" artists again from 1925 to 1929 at The Intimate Gallery, a small space in a commercial art auction gallery on Park Avenue at 59th Street, and after that closed, at An American Place, a rented space on the seventeenth floor of a modern skyscraper at Madison Avenue and 53rd Street. The rebellious spirit of his gallery is expressed by the card Stieglitz had printed to express his intentions. There would be "*No* formal press views; *No* cocktail parties; *No* special invitations; *No* advertising; *No* institutions; *No* isms; *No* theories; *No* games being played; *Nothing* asked of anyone who comes; No *anything* on the walls except what *you see there*." And furthermore, "*The doors of An American Place are ever open to all*." Besides expressing what Stieglitz believed was right, this card certainly notified one and all what he believed wrong with other galleries. He was so enamored of O'Keeffe's work that he was reluctant to sell it, although shows of her new work became a yearly event, and every year it had new impact, surprising and even shocking critics. "We have petitioned the fire commissioner to allow us to paint our running gear red and to carry a clanging bell," wrote a *New Yorker* critic on the opening of her 1926 exhibition. "We will then tear through the streets, hoping that many will follow. . . . For if ever there were a raging, blazing soul mounting to the skies it is that of Georgia O'Keeffe. . . .

Below: Georgia O'Keeffe and art collector Mrs. Chester Dale converse at a preview in New York City, January, 1940.

Right: Completed in 1982, O'Keeffe's 10-foot-high sculpture, titled *Abstraction*, was cast and painted aluminum.

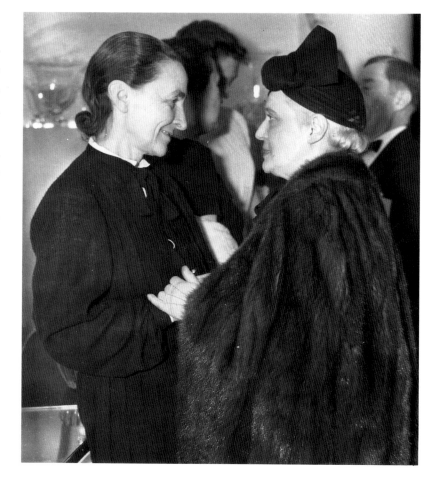

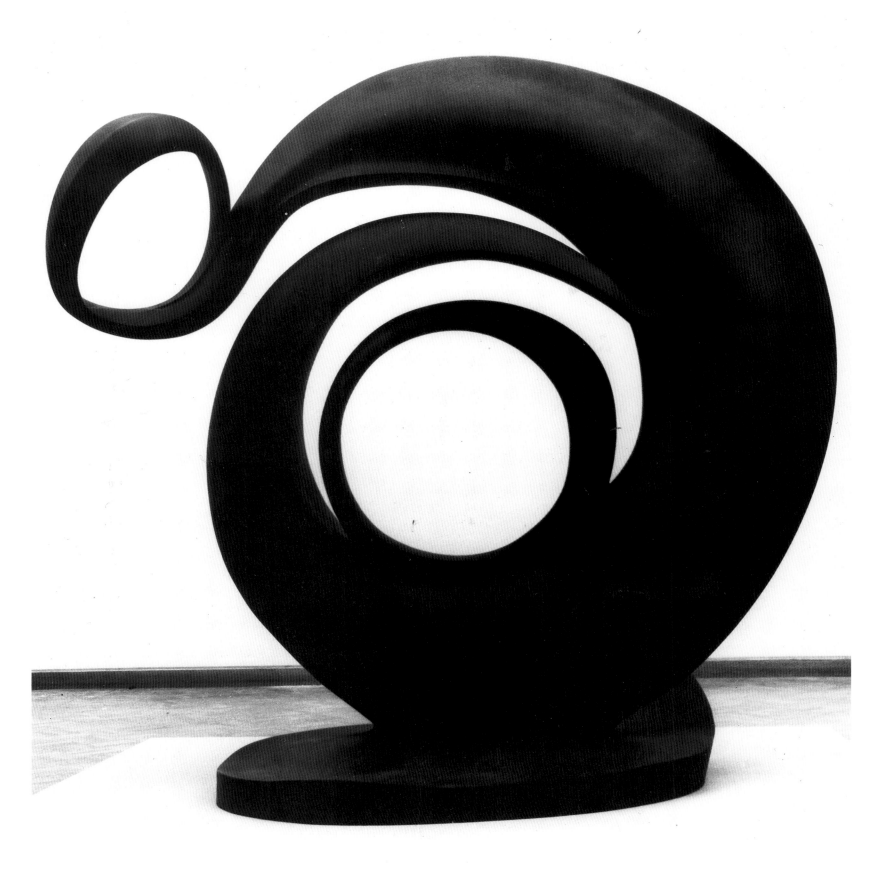

One O'Keeffe hung in Grand Central Station would even halt the home-going commuters . . . surely if the authorities knew they would pass laws against Georgia O'Keeffe, take away her magic tubes and brushes."

In 1924 O'Keeffe began to paint flowers as they had never been painted before. She drew in as close to them as a bee, and sometimes painted only parts of the whole. She spoke about her impetus being to make people pay attention, to see flowers as she saw them. People did pay attention. They were shocked. The cognoscenti, who came to see them exhibited in 1926, looked through Freud-tinted glasses. Then it was O'Keeffe's turn to be shocked, or, at least, annoyed. She took to telling

people who saw sexual symbols that they were seeing their own obsessions.

It is notable that, after she and Stieglitz started to live together, O'Keeffe almost never painted people. It has been said she was simply not interested. She has said that she wouldn't want to put anyone else through the physical discomfort of posing that she had to endure. When he began making his images of her, Stieglitz used glass plates and she had to remain still for three minutes at a time – over and over again. "He photographed me 'till I was crazy," she said.

There is another reason she may have shunned painting people. After her year at the Art Students League she re-

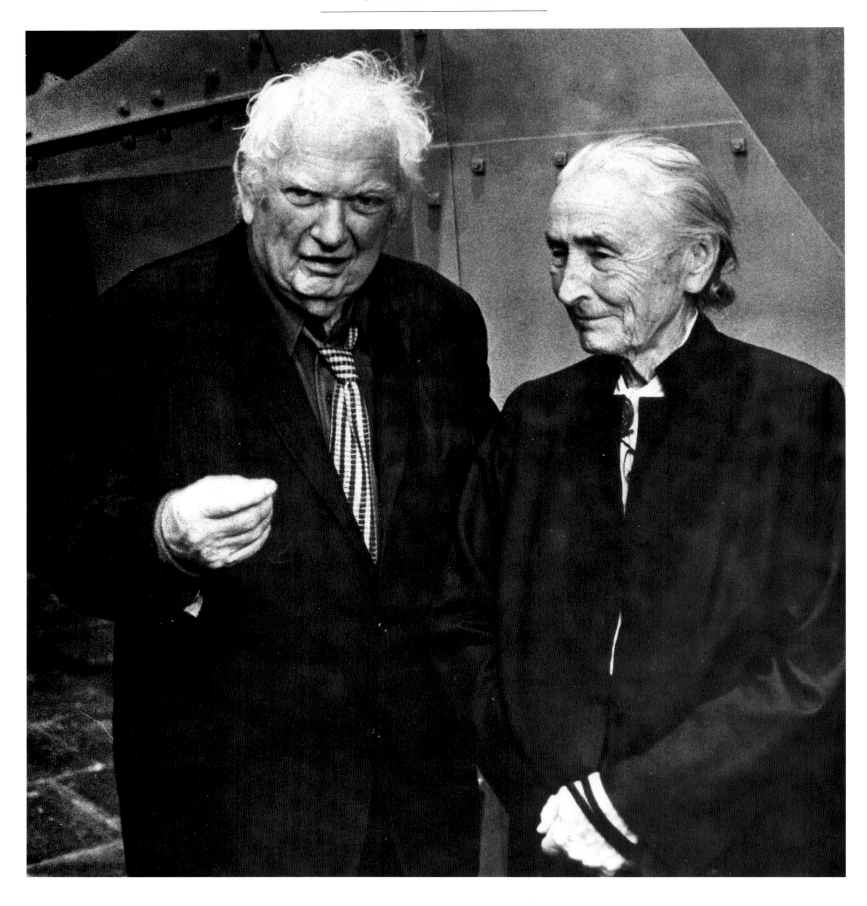

nounced a career in art because, looking at all her own work, she could identify the influence of others. Besides wanting to be independent and paint as an expression of her own life, she found no point in trying to do what great painters had done before her. Similarly, she must have believed that she could never capture the truth and character of people as Stieglitz did, and there was no point in trying.

Although Stieglitz was quick to champion her first abstractions, his immediate reaction to her big flowers was, "Well, what are you going to do with those?" When she began painting cityscapes in the mid-1920s, she again met resistance from him

and from the other men in the group. It was all very well for her to paint flowers, by then, but not the city. Why, she was told, even the men couldn't do that very well. She held firm. "From my teens I had been told I had crazy notions so I was accustomed to disagreement and went on with my idea of painting New York."

She used to enjoy recounting how she painted one dull picture of a building, a shanty at Lake George, New York, just for fun. It was a brown, shabby building scorched by the sun, that was eventually fixed up for her to work in. In her picture she made it "all low-toned and dreary" so that it would look like the

22

"dismal-colored paintings" the men did. When it went up in her next show, they approved. It was bought for The Phillips Collection in Washington, D.C., but it was the only such gloomy work she ever did.

O'Keeffe and Stieglitz had a complicated relationship. He began to photograph her soon after they met and continued to do so with ardent, sensual, erotic, obsessive pleasure. He explored every mood and every inch of her being with self-indulgent passion. No comparable portrait of any woman has ever been made. Artistically they had deep respect, mutual appreciation and admiration for one another's work. Sometimes friendly competition entered into their endeavors when he photographed and she painted the same subject. They were mesmerized by each other. "I had a need of him that I had never seemed to feel for anyone else before," she told Anita Pollitzer. "His feeling for music, concerts, books and the outdoors was wonderful. He would notice shapes and colors different from those I had seen and so delicate that I began to notice more."

The gap in their ages was significant, but even more so – and

Left: Georgia O'Keeffe and sculptor Alexander Calder chat at a dinner honoring Calder at the Whitney Museum of American Art in 1976.

Below: Juan Hamilton, O'Keeffe's companion and assistant from 1976 until her death in 1986, is pictured in November, 1986.

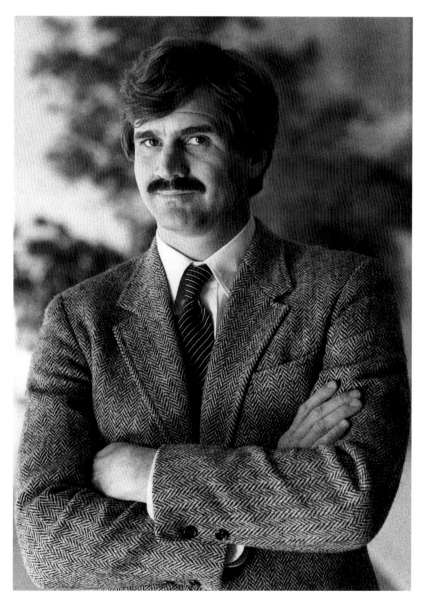

what came to be divisive – was the vast difference in the way each liked to live his or her life. Stieglitz enjoyed and thrived on being surrounded by people. He loved conversation – heated, elaborate, opinionated discussion – especially when he had a good audience. He disliked travel and was content to live in New York City and, in the summers, at his family's retreat at Lake George, New York. Georgia O'Keeffe preferred a more solitary life. She disliked the conversations that went on and on, often into the morning hours. They seemed irrelevant. They bored her. She liked to travel. She felt suffocated by the crowds at the Lake George compound. The landscape at the lake held no particular appeal for her, although she painted many wonderful pictures there. As she later remarked, it was, "Very pretty. But it wasn't made for me." Nor was she happy to be in the city, although there, too, she painted views that stopped people in their tracks. It was as though she was waiting for a chance to get back to the open plains of Texas, or, better still, as it turned out, New Mexico.

It was in 1929 that O'Keeffe began spending her summers in New Mexico, first with a friend and later in a place of her own. She had already been to Santa Fe, 11 years earlier, as part of a vacation trip she had taken with her sister. It stayed in her mind as the place to which she wished to return. If the windy plains of Texas had been her country before, the isolation, the vast empty spaces, the hard dry earth, dramatic hills and desert landscape, the Indian dances and wildflowers of northern New Mexico now became her place.

She could never persuade Stieglitz to join her in New Mexico, and he could never persuade her to give it up. When she rejoined him at Lake George one year, she packed a barrel full of the bleached bones and skulls she had been gathering on the desert and took them East to paint during the winter. To seekers of deep symbolism they were a reflection of death. To O'Keeffe they were lively images.

Tension in her life increased because the direction of her passionate artistic interest was diverging from that which Stieglitz wished. Both strong characters, they fought one another, if not outright, in battles of will. He became interested in a young woman, Dorothy Norman, who started visiting his gallery in 1926. O'Keeffe accepted a commission to paint a mural at Radio City Music Hall in 1932, against Stieglitz's wishes. That added to the strain and, when the project itself was complicated by technical problems, she reneged on the contract and later, as the anxiety overwhelmed her, she had a nervous breakdown. Stieglitz, who had lost his position of great magnetism and power in the art world, became more feeble, and O'Keeffe, once her own health was better, spent a good deal of time nursing him. He had a major coronary, followed by pneumonia in 1938, and then in the next years had a series of angina attacks before he died in July of 1946.

Stieglitz was 82 years old when he died. O'Keeffe was not quite 59. She spent the next two years settling his estate, helping to prepare a show of his personal art collection at the Museum of Modern Art, in 1947, and organizing and dispersing

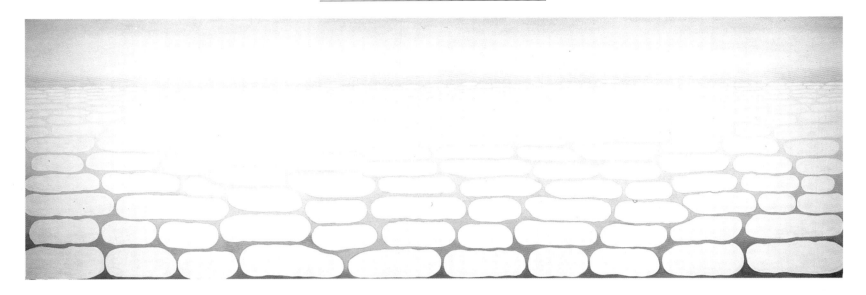

the entire collection. In 1949 she settled permanently in New Mexico. She also began to travel widely, in Mexico, South America and Europe. In 1959 she went to the Far East, Southeast Asia, India, the Middle East and Italy. The next year she went to Japan, Formosa, the Philippines, Hong Kong, Southeast Asia and the Pacific Islands. In 1963 she traveled to Greece, Egypt and the Near East. During those years several shows of her work were also organized, and she received many honors. In 1965 she painted her largest work ever, an astounding 8-by-24-feet regimented parade of clouds in a work entitled *Sky Above Clouds*.

In January 1963 O'Keeffe was visited by a British poet, Charles Tomlinson, who found her house behind a long low wall and a gateway adorned by an immense deer skull. "When I admired the trophy at the gate later that afternoon, she replied, 'I swapped a hi-fi set for it,'" he recalled in his memoir. She was 75 then. She lived as simply but elegantly as ever, surrounded by stark white walls. Flowerless grey twigs were held in black vases made at a nearby pueblo, animal bones of various sizes and smooth, round stones rested on ledges and tables. There were Chinese statues and African masks for decoration but absolutely no paintings by O'Keeffe and no photographs by Stieglitz.

"I had no great passions. I went my own way. I didn't even intend to 'live' by painting because there's the danger that you'll try to copy the style of someone else and 'work' it," she told Tomlinson. And as to her New Mexico home she said, "The clarity, that's what I love about this place."

In 1971 she suffered the loss of her central vision and had to stop painting. Yet, Georgia O'Keeffe's spirit seemed not to flag. In 1976 a young man with long hair – an eccentricity that amused and delighted O'Keeffe – came to work for her. He was a potter named Juan Hamilton and he taught her how to build clay pots by hand. Hamilton became her traveling companion as well as her assistant in such work as a book, *Georgia O'Keeffe*, with over 100 of her pictures and her own comments about them. "She is one of the most lively, energetic human beings I've ever met," this young man said about her in 1976.

George O'Keeffe died in March of 1986 at the age of 98. With the anticlimax of a bad movie – and a fate that seems en-

Above: O'Keeffe's last major work, *Sky Above the Clouds VI*, was a colossal one, measuring 8-by-24-feet. She completed this celestial scene in 1965. (The Art Institute of Chicago, Illinois)

Right: A photo portrait of Georgia O'Keeffe, taken in 1970, when she was 83 years old.

demic to artists' estates – a nasty probate dispute between Juan Hamilton, who inherited most of her property, and O'Keeffe relatives went on for nearly a year. Her estate was valued at over $65 million.

The 1987 retrospective traveling exhibition of O'Keeffe's work, organized by the National Gallery of Art, aimed to show the paintings considered to have most affected our art and vision. Jack Cowart, head of the department and curator of twentieth-century art at the Gallery, and Juan Hamilton selected the works in the exhibition. The idea of the person is larger than life, since her personality rather than her art was the focus of attention for many years, said Cowart. "O'Keeffe herself is at least partially responsible for this situation," he wrote in the catalogue. "As she grew older especially, O'Keeffe knew she filled a void in American art, that her images were becoming icons, and that her deportment was legendary. Events conspired to produce for the public not an informed awareness but a stark cliché, a stereotype."

Critics are still divided in their estimations of her work and probably always will be. Tributes that called her our greatest living woman painter stopped short of calling her our greatest living painter. And, of course, some critics were, and are, not enthusiastic. Writing in *The Nation* in 1946, Clement Greenberg slashed: ". . . the greatest part of her work adds up to little more than tinted photography . . . less to do with art than with private worship and the embellishment of private fetishes with secret and arbitrary meanings." Forty-two years later Kay Larson wrote in *New York* magazine about the 1987 O'Keeffe exhibition, "O'Keeffe is a good artist, but the word 'great' weighs her down like a cross."

If we look at Georgia O'Keeffe as closely as she looked at beautiful flowers, we may find that the more we magnify a part, the less we are able to see the whole flower. But it also may be that, in a moment of clairvoyance, one detail seen very, very

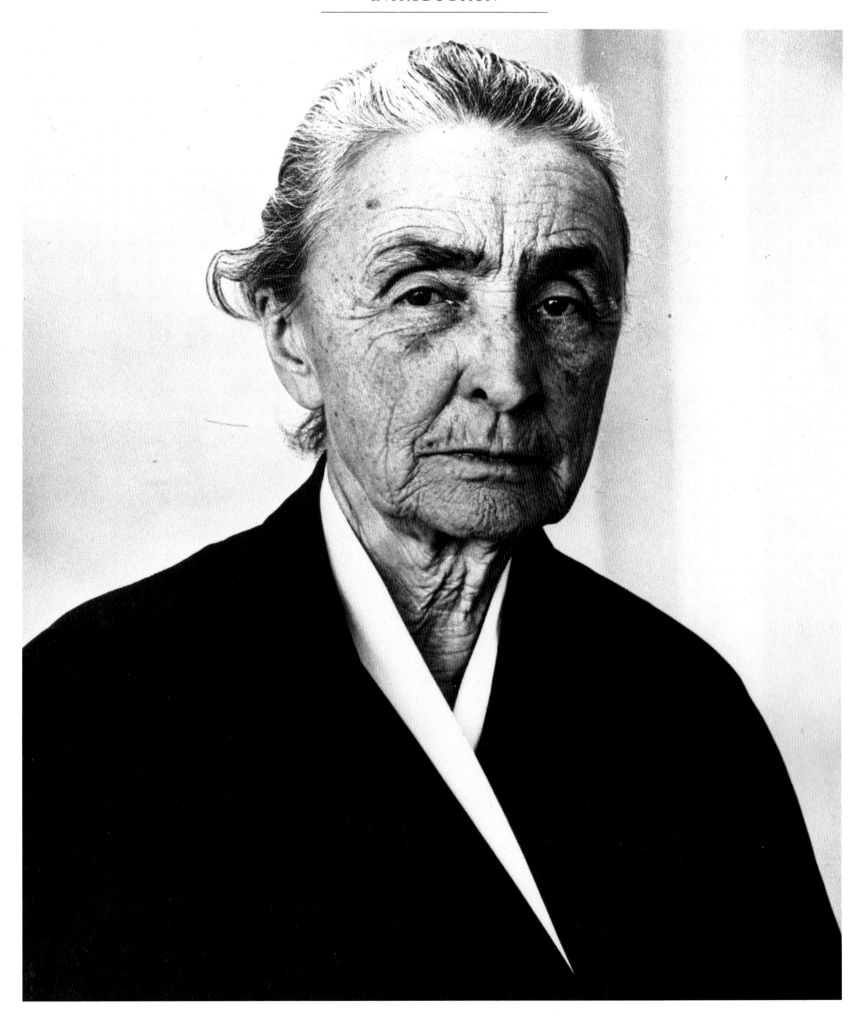

well, may reveal the entire plant. This much is true: she was a talented, bold, exciting, extraordinary, innovative artist, and it is hard to know what else is needed to call her great.

Georgia O'Keeffe was born before the beginnings of Modern Art, and kept her own voice through the hundreds of "isms" that have been attached to each new movement that followed on the heels of the pioneers. Certainly she was influenced by her contemporaries as well as her predecessors, and she, in turn, has influenced innumerable artists of her own era and later. Above all she was – finally, controversially – above all.

25

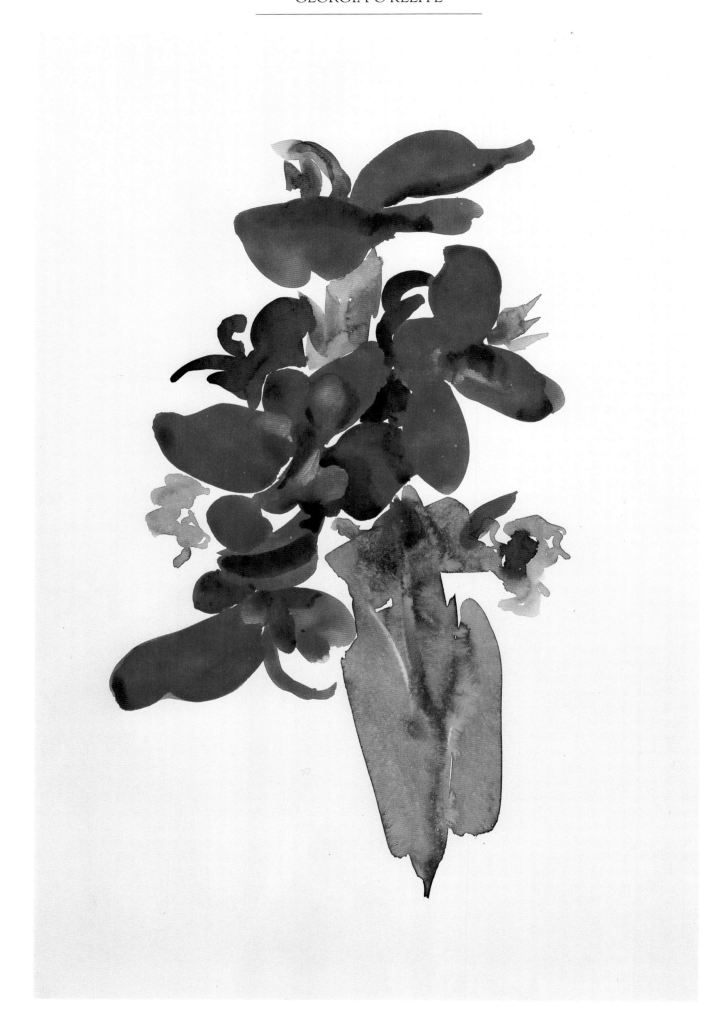

Red Canna
c. 1920, watercolor on paper, 19⅜×13 in.
Gift of George Hooper Fitch, B.A. 1932,
and Mrs. Fitch,
Yale University Art Gallery, New Haven, CT

NATURE IN FOCUS

There are a few objects in nature that Georgia O'Keeffe looked at with unusually intense concentration: flowers, shells and animal skeletons among them. O'Keeffe painted flowers with an impact no one else had ever achieved. She began in 1924 and, in the catalogue introducing those images she wrote, "Everyone has many associations with a flower. You put out your hand to touch it, or lean forward to smell it, or maybe touch it with your lips almost without thinking, or give it to someone to please them. But one rarely takes the time to really see a flower. I have painted what each flower is to me and I have painted it big enough so that others will see what I see."

In her lifetime O'Keeffe painted flowers over 200 times. When asked why she made them so large she answered, "But you don't ask me why I make the river so small." Her intention was to follow in the tradition of Oriental artists whose flowers express their moods. Consider also that she looked at flowers very much as Stieglitz looked at her. He framed her face, her hands, he focused on the most intimate parts of her body, often microscopically, and studied each detail as though the whole world resided there. O'Keeffe did that using a flower instead of a person.

It can be argued that Georgia O'Keeffe has made the brilliant red poppy the most famous single flower in America – next to Vincent Van Gogh's sunflowers, perhaps the most famous flower in the Western world. In fact, she painted poppies many times, although the one we are most familiar with was painted in 1927, it did not achieve celebrity until 1987, the year after O'Keeffe's death, when it became the advertising and poster art for a major, traveling exhibition of her work. Before that O'Keeffe was more widely known for her skull paintings, which had illustrated catalogue covers. But few people who went to the 1987 exhibition, after seeing the poppy in ads and on posters, failed to be surprised. Instead of a heroically large canvas, as many of her flower paintings are, it is just about 7-by-9-inches. That's a miniature compared to the University of Minnesota's *Oriental Poppies*, which measures 3 feet 4 inches wide, or the single *Poppy* owned by the Museum of Fine Arts in St. Petersburg, Florida, which is 3-by-2½-feet.

The gossip, if not scandal, caused by the presumed sexual innuendo in these flower paintings is all very well if one is prepared to say that anything provocative enough to draw attention to fine art can't be all bad. The trouble is that such interpretation can be as blinding as looking into the sun. Once these flowers begin to seem like genitalia, is difficult to forget that and look at them for emotion, mood, form, color, texture, light and other significant details the artist used to express her experience of the flower.

Artists of many centuries painted flowers before Georgia O'Keeffe did. There were still lifes in the *Vanitas* vein – works that revealed the "vanity" and transitory nature of beauty and life. Flowers were also painted for their mystical and folkloric symbolism. Although no one was quite so bold as she, many men who painted flowers both before and while she did (including the Americans Martin Johnson Heade in the nineteenth century and Charles Demuth, Joseph Stella and Jim Dine in the twentieth) also painted them close-up and enlarged. Theirs, however, were not viewed with shocked interpretation as erotic symbols, intentional or otherwise.

After gleefully superimposing unintended meaning on her flowers, commentators have also had a field day with the skulls and bones she began to paint in 1931 – symbols of death of course, they insisted. After all, skulls are traditional *Vanitas* symbols, as any student of art history soon finds out. But O'Keeffe's skulls were extraordinary objects in and of themselves. She rejected the morbid metaphor and insisted that, to her, they were very lively indeed. The story she told about one cow's skull, white painted against a background of red and blue, is that it was a joke on the men who were always talking about "the Great American Novel, the Great American Play, the Great American Everything," as she put it. "I thought they didn't know anything about America. They never went across the Hudson!" So, as a mischievous parody, she framed her skull as a patriotic emblem. But, they didn't get it.

As for the symbolic juxtaposition of life (flowers) and death (skull) in, for instance the marvellous *Cow's Skull with Calico Roses*, in truth the flowers are artificial. The combination evolved one day at Lake George when someone came to the door and, going to see who it was, she thoughtlessly stuck a flower she'd been looking at in the eye socket of a skull she had brought with her from New Mexico. Later, looking at the bizarre combination, she found it amusing and attractive.

As the artist Charles Demuth said about O'Keeffe's paintings, "In her canvases each color almost regains the fun it must have had within itself on forming the first rainbow." While it is probably not a sin to over-interpret works of art while looking for symbol and metaphor, the great harm is that pleasure to the senses might get lost in the mental calisthenics. Whatever they suggest beyond their immediate reality, she studied flowers, shells and bones as nature's objects of art – and painted them as her own.

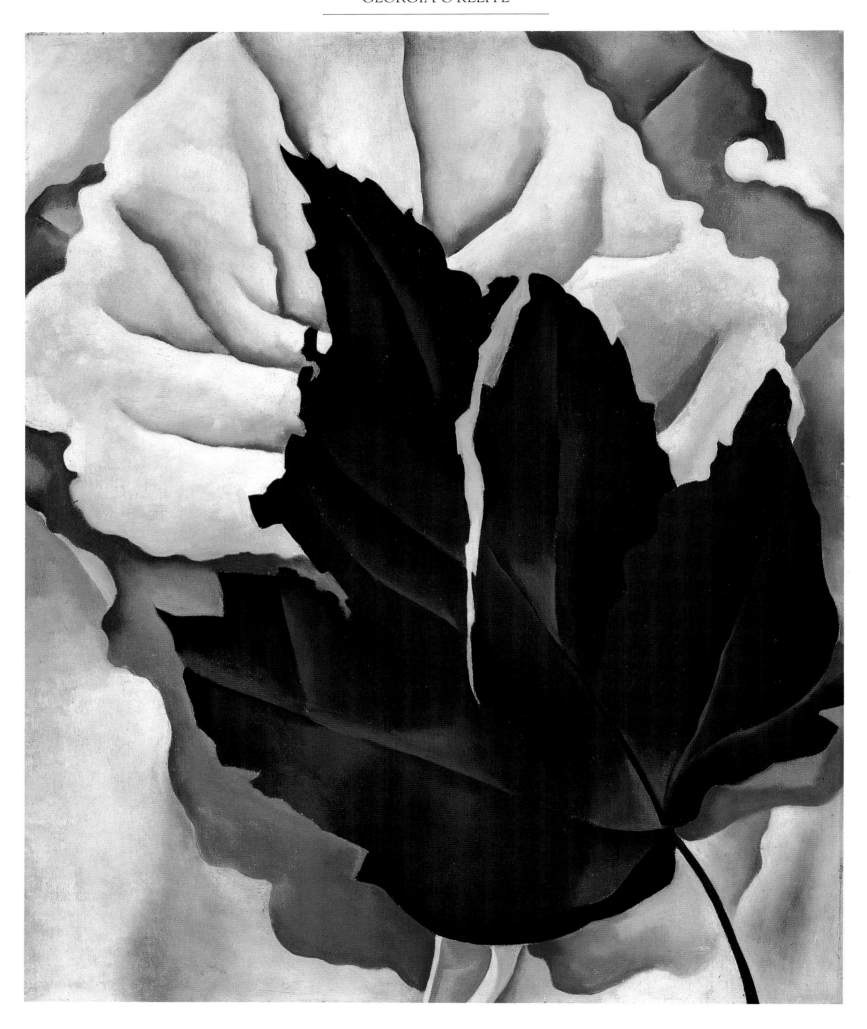

Pattern of Leaves
c. 1923, oil on canvas, 22⅛ × 18⅛ in.
Acquired 1926,
The Phillips Collection, Washington, D.C.

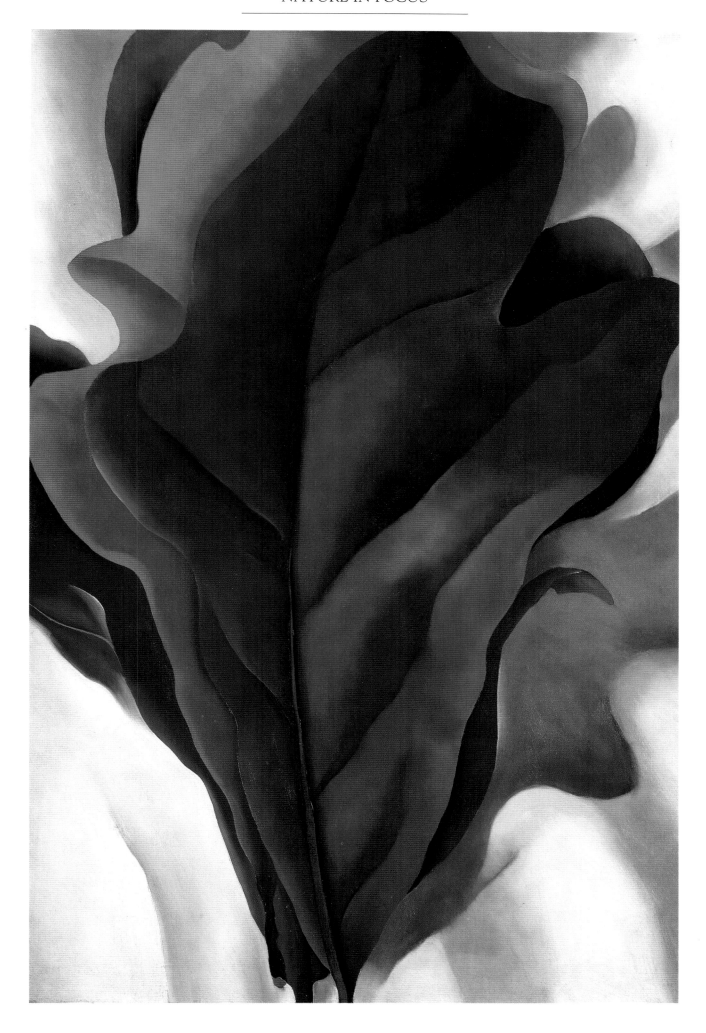

Large Dark Red Leaves on White
1925, oil on canvas, 32×21 in.
Acquired 1943,
The Phillips Collection, Washington, D.C.

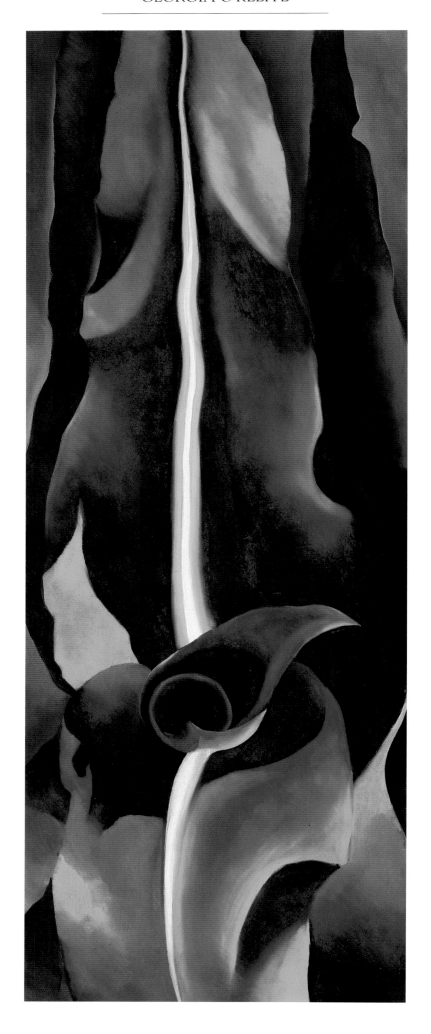

Corn Dark, I
1924, oil on composition board, 31¾×11⅞ in.
The Alfred Stieglitz Collection, 1950,
The Metropolitan Museum of Art, New York, NY
(50.236.1)

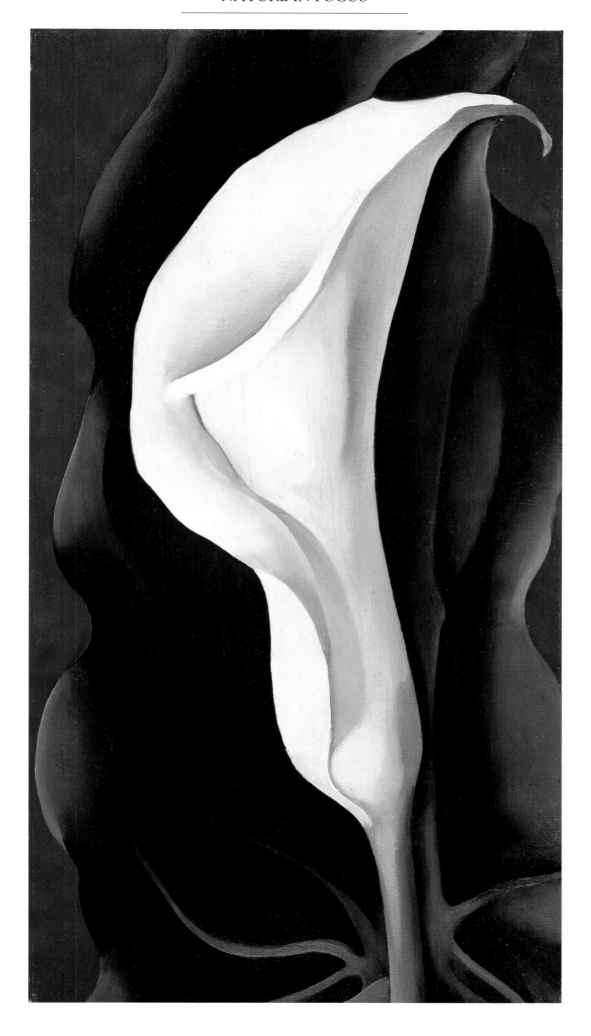

Single Lily with Red
1928, oil on wood, 12×6¼ in.
Purchase 33.29,
Whitney Museum of American Art, New York, NY

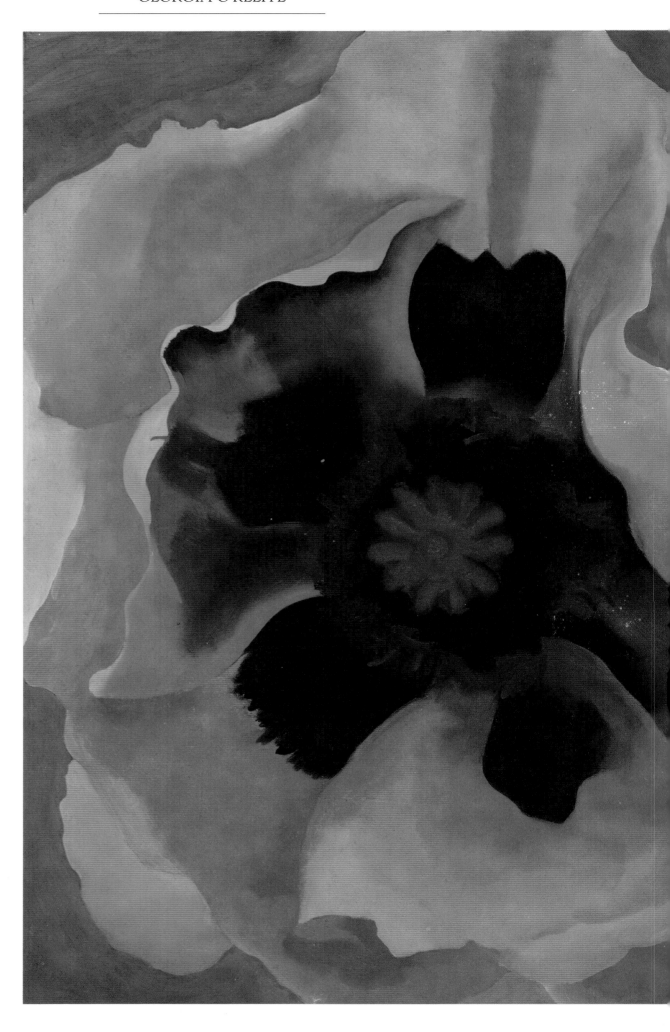

Oriental Poppies
1928, oil on canvas, 30×40⅛ in.
University Art Museum,
University of Minnesota, Minneapolis
(37.1)

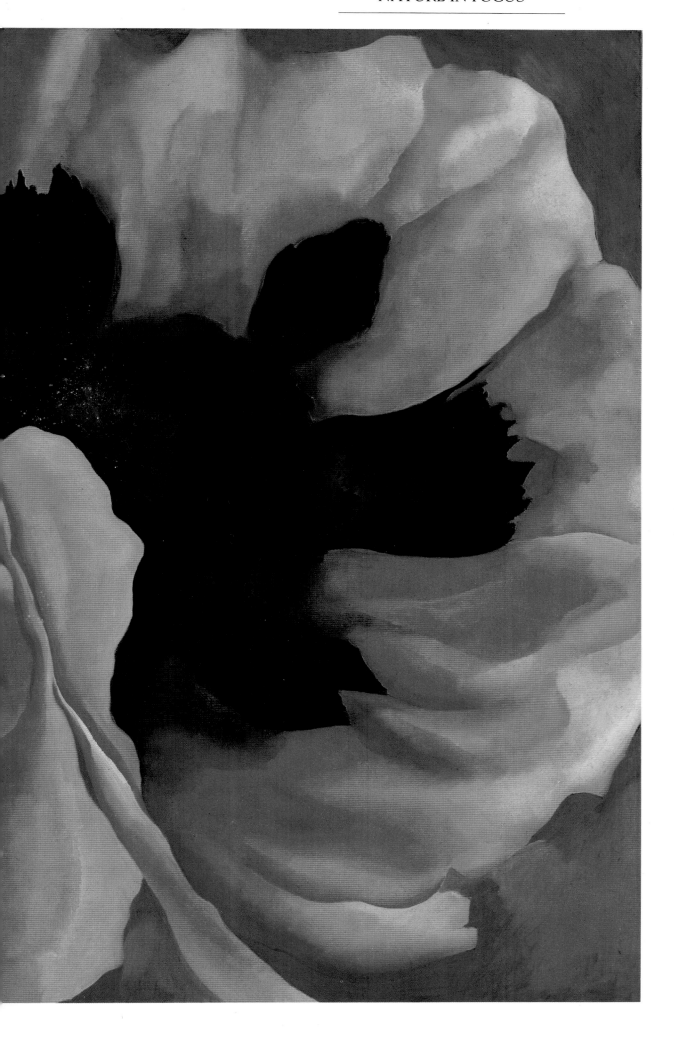

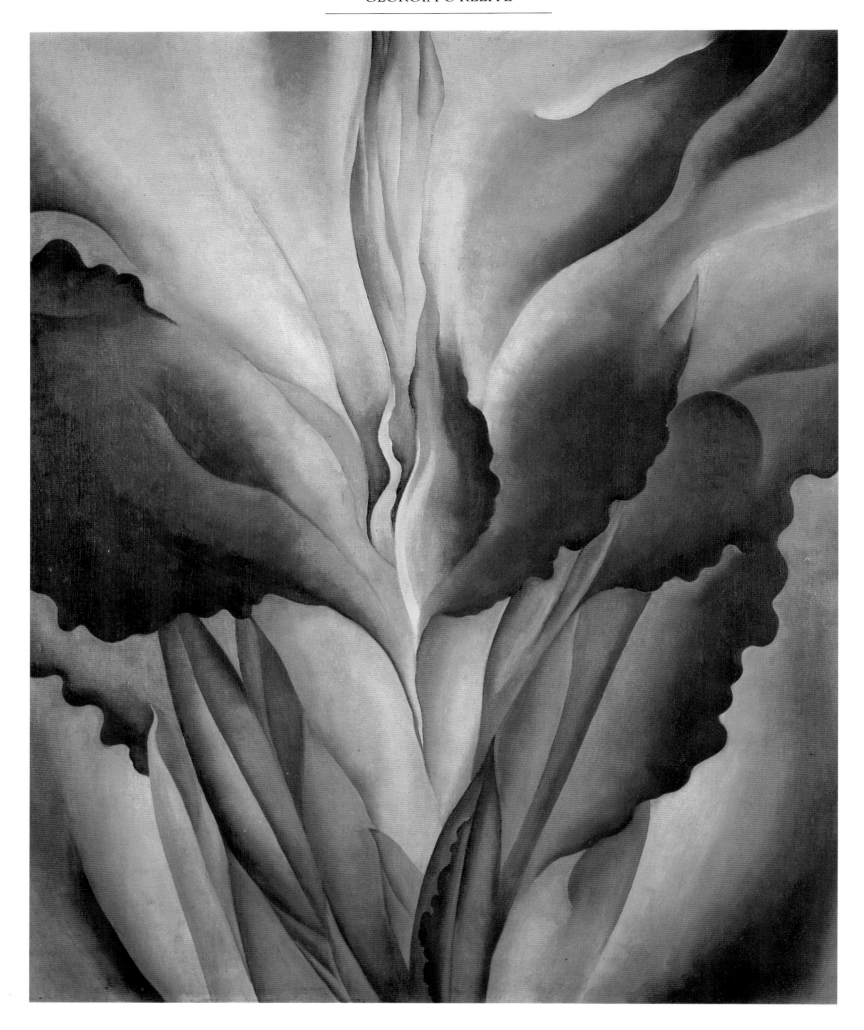

Red Canna
c. 1924, oil on canvas mounted on masonite,
36×29⅞ in.
Gift of Oliver James,
University of Arizona Museum of Art, Tucson, AZ

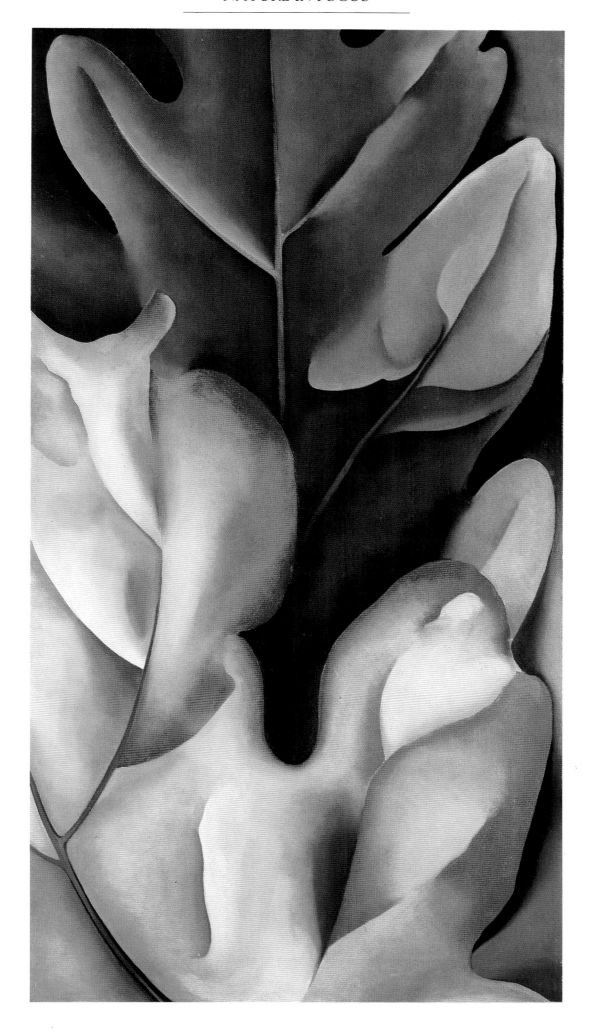

Oak Leaves – Pink and Gray
1929, oil on canvas, 33⅛×18 in.
General Budget Fund, 1936,
University Gallery, University of Minnesota,
Minneapolis
(36.85)

Narcissa's Last Orchid
1941, pastel, 21⅜×27⅛ in.
Gift of David H. McAlpin,
The Art Museum, Princeton University,
Princeton, NJ

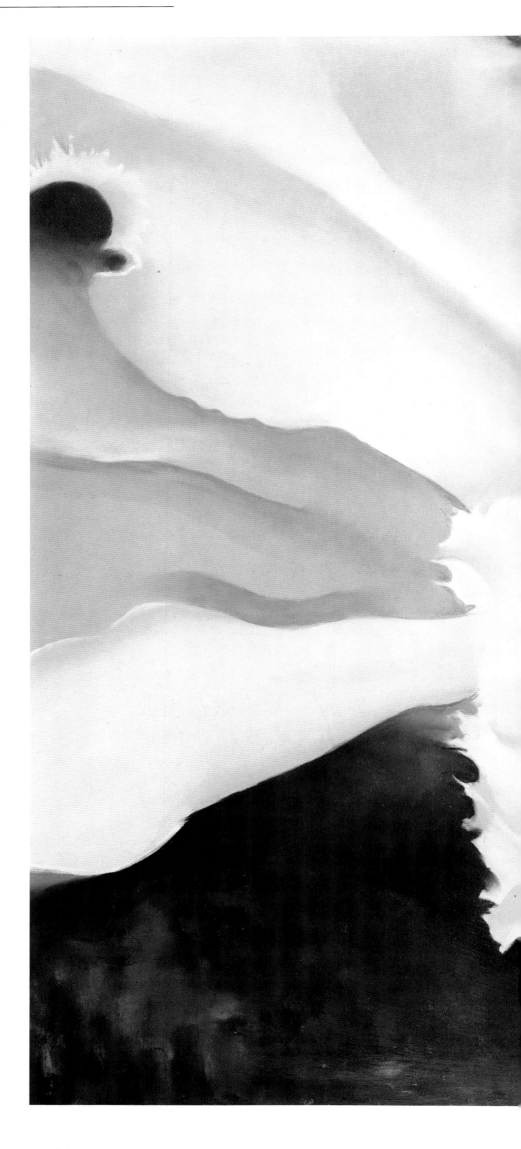

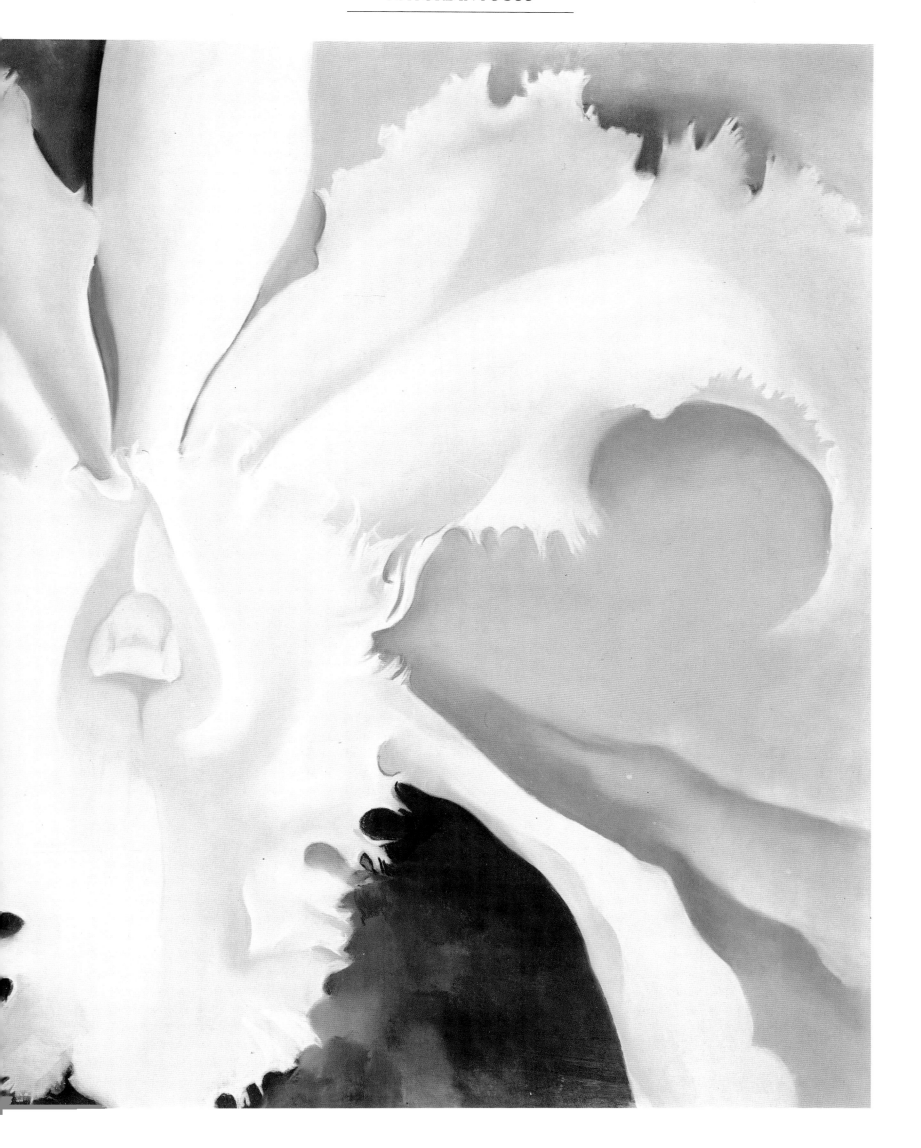

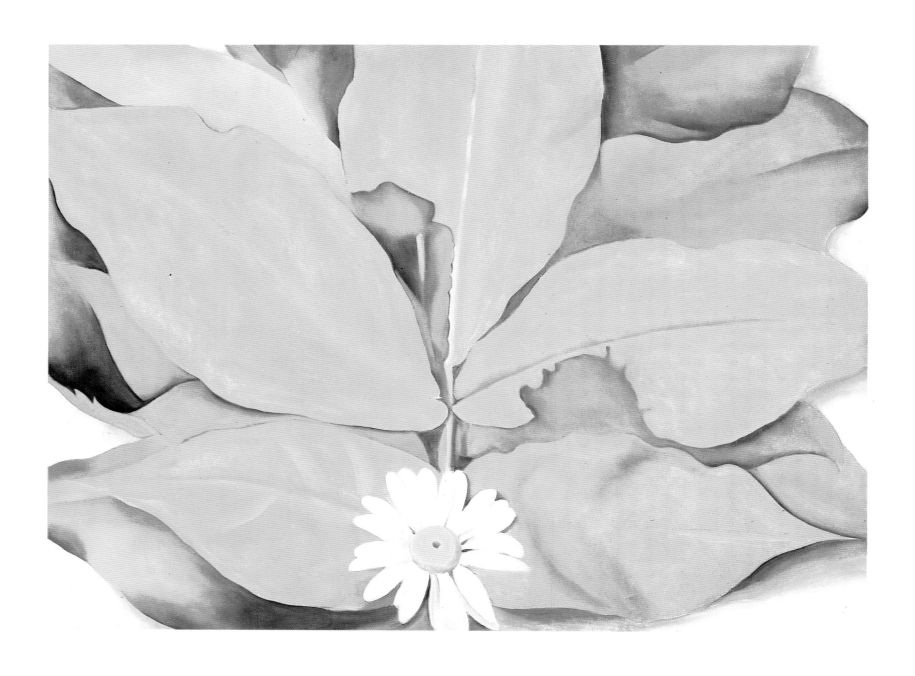

Yellow Hickory Leaves with Daisy
1928, oil on canvas, 29¾×39¾ in.
Gift of Georgia O'Keeffe to the
Alfred Stieglitz Collection, 1965,
The Art Institute of Chicago, Chicago, IL

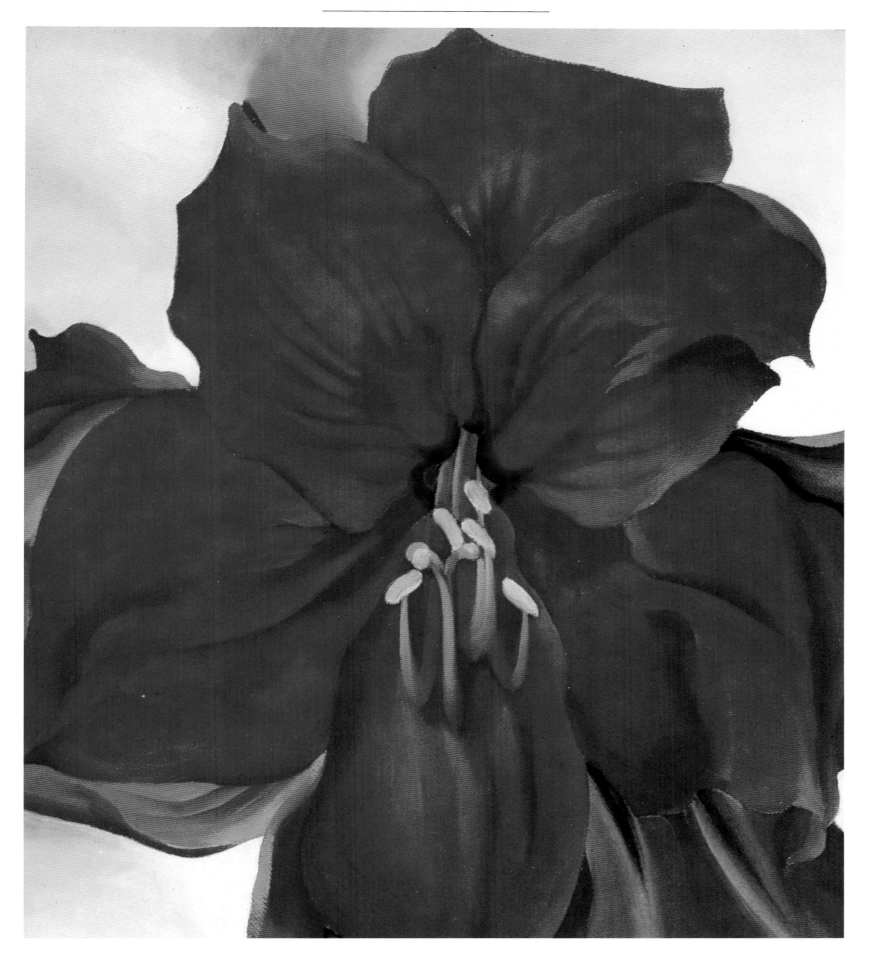

Red Amaryllis
n.d., oil on canvas, 11⅞×10 in.
Gift of Mrs. Henrietta Roig,
Terra Museum of American Art, Chicago, IL

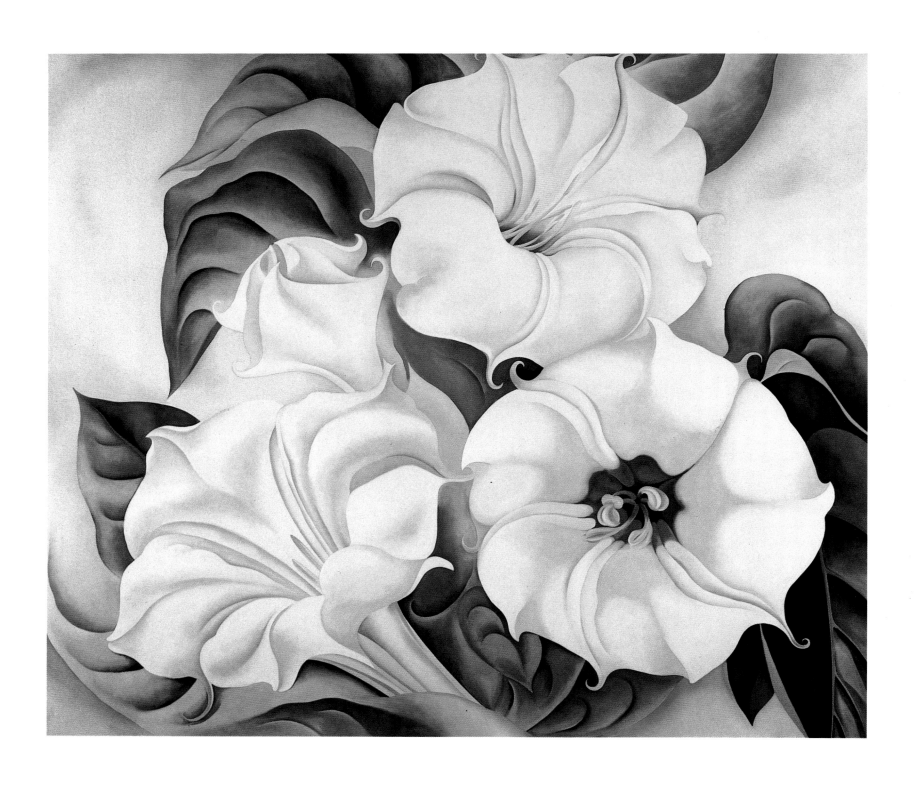

Jimsonweed
1936, oil on canvas, 70×83½ in.
On loan from Eli Lilly & Company,
Indianapolis Museum of Art, Indianapolis, IN
(TR 6623)

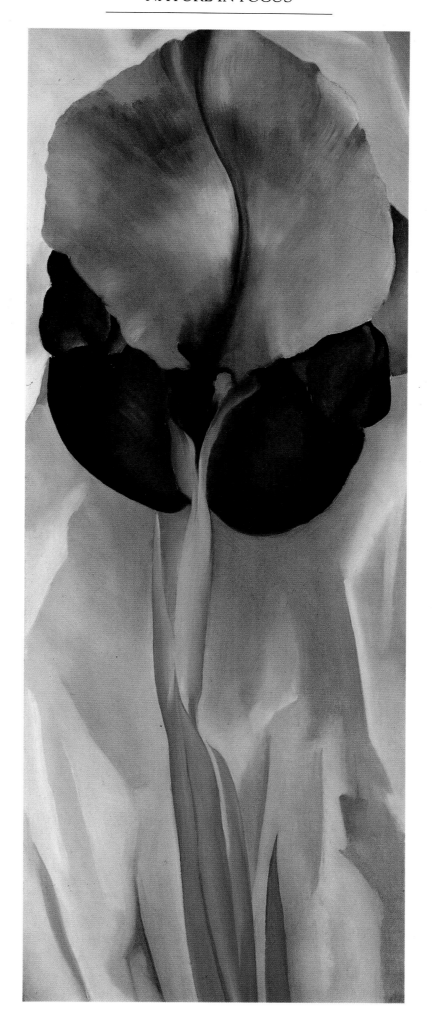

Iris
1929, oil on canvas 32×12 in.
Anonymous gift,
Colorado Springs Fine Arts Center

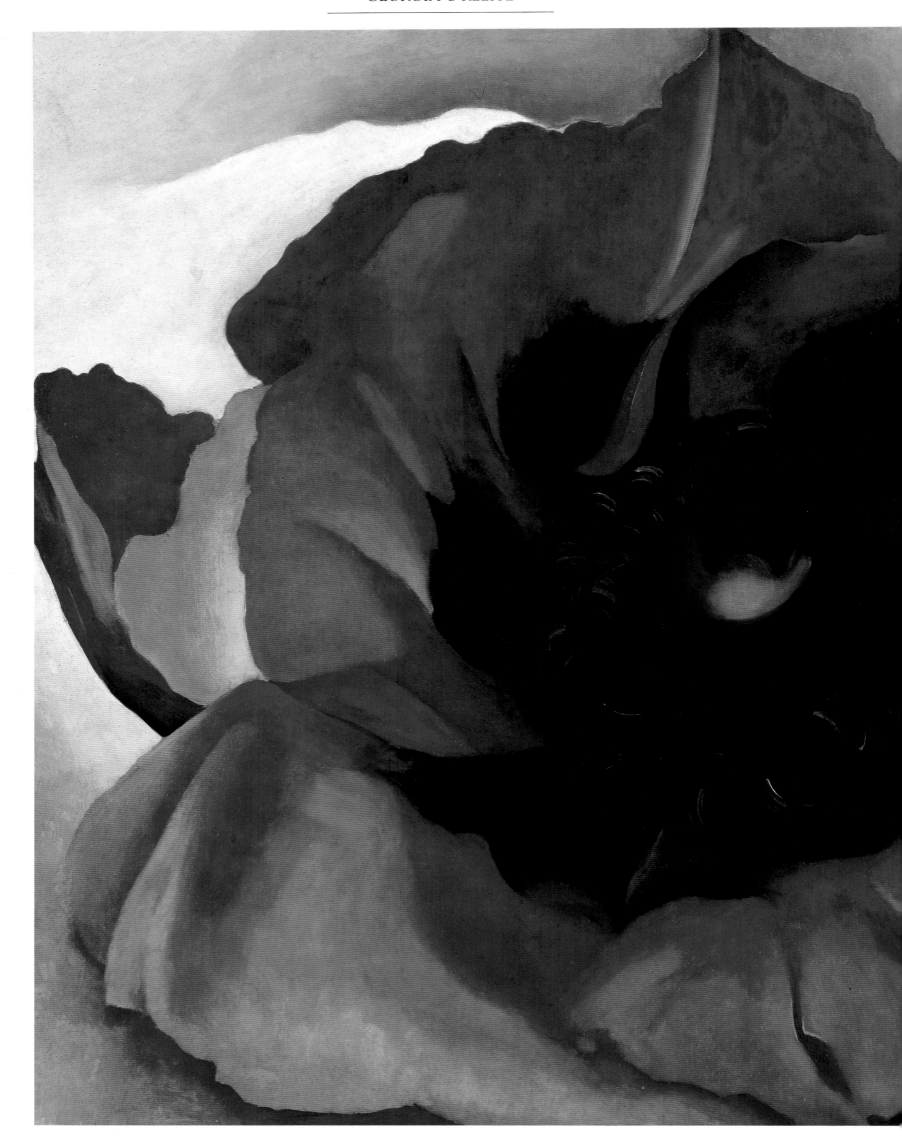

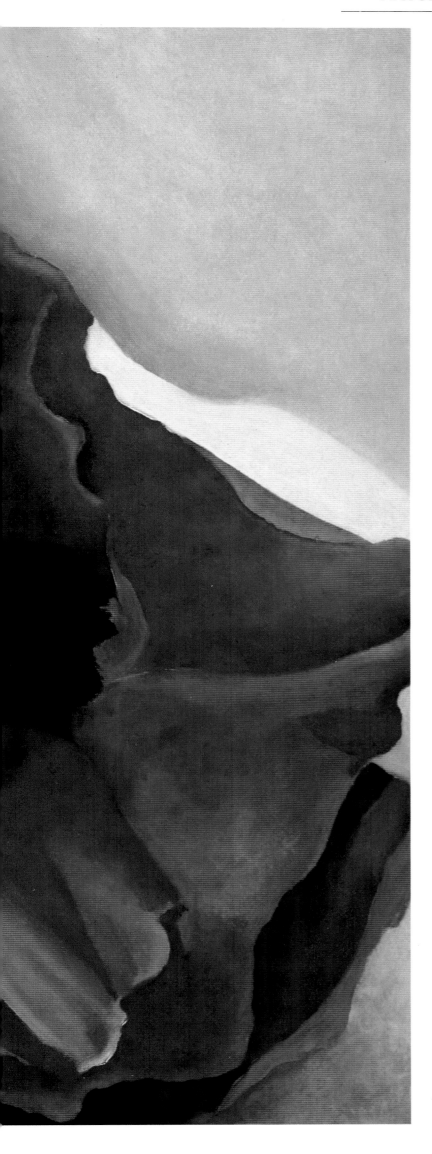

Poppy
1927, oil on canvas, 30×36 in.
*Gift of Charles C. and Margaret Stevenson
Henderson in memory of Hunt Henderson,
Museum of Fine Arts, St. Petersburg, FL*

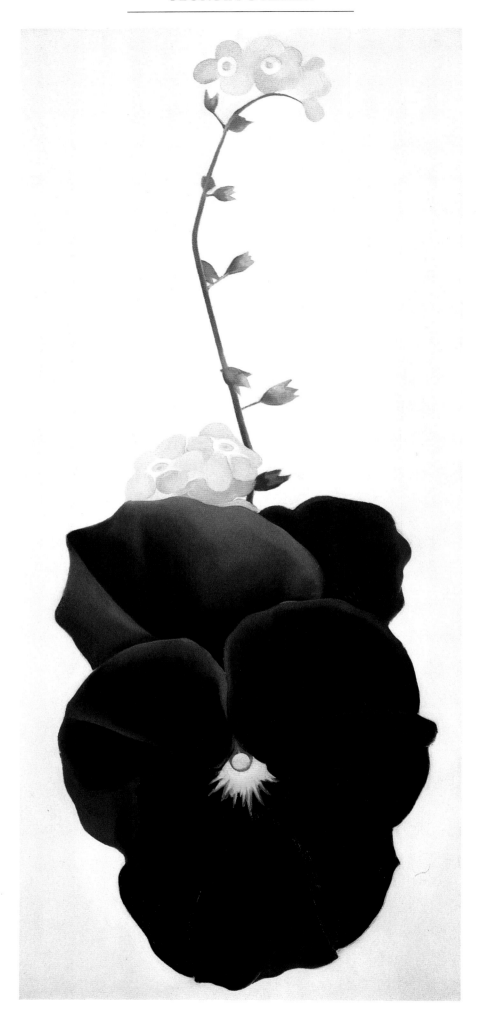

Pansy
1926, oil on canvas, 26¹⁵⁄₁₆×12¹⁄₁₆ in.
Gift of Mrs. Alfred S. Rossin,
The Brooklyn Museum, Brooklyn, NY
(28.521)

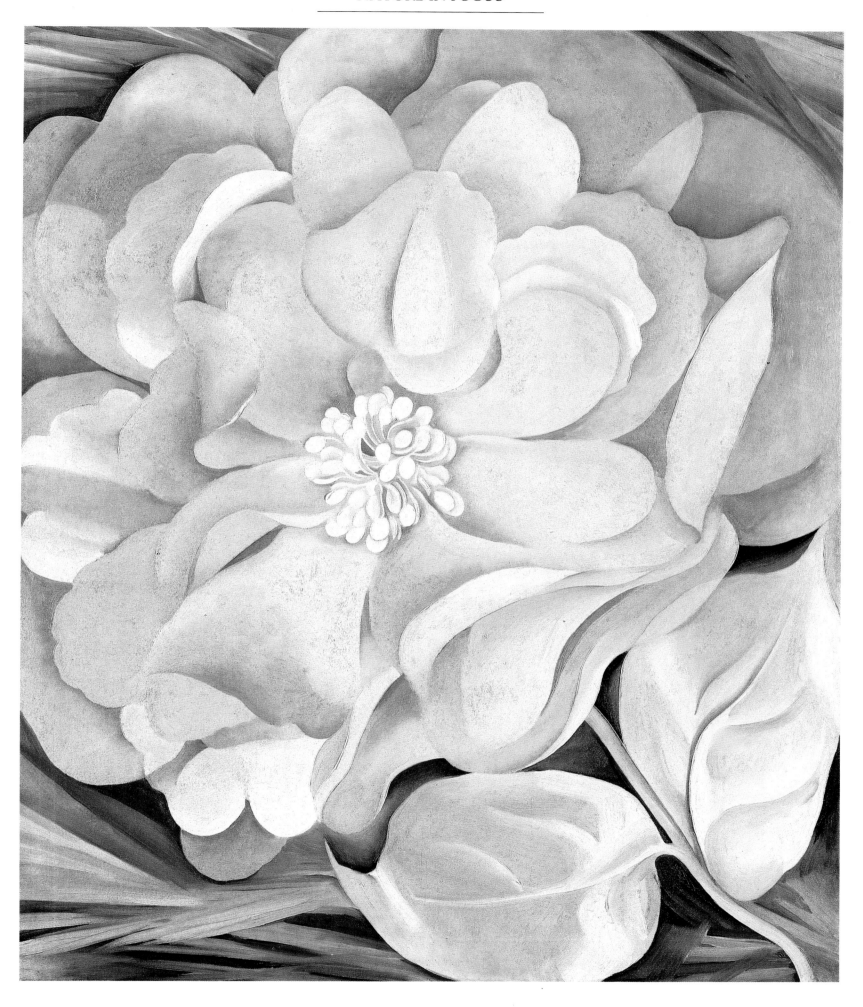

The White Calico Flower
1931, oil on canvas, 30×36 in.
Purchase 32.26,
Collection of Whitney Museum of American Art,
New York, NY

Overleaf:
Pink and Yellow Hollyhocks
1952, oil on canvas, 24×40 in.
Bequest of Helen Miller Jones,
Marion Koogler McNay Art Museum,
San Antonio, TX
(1989.37)

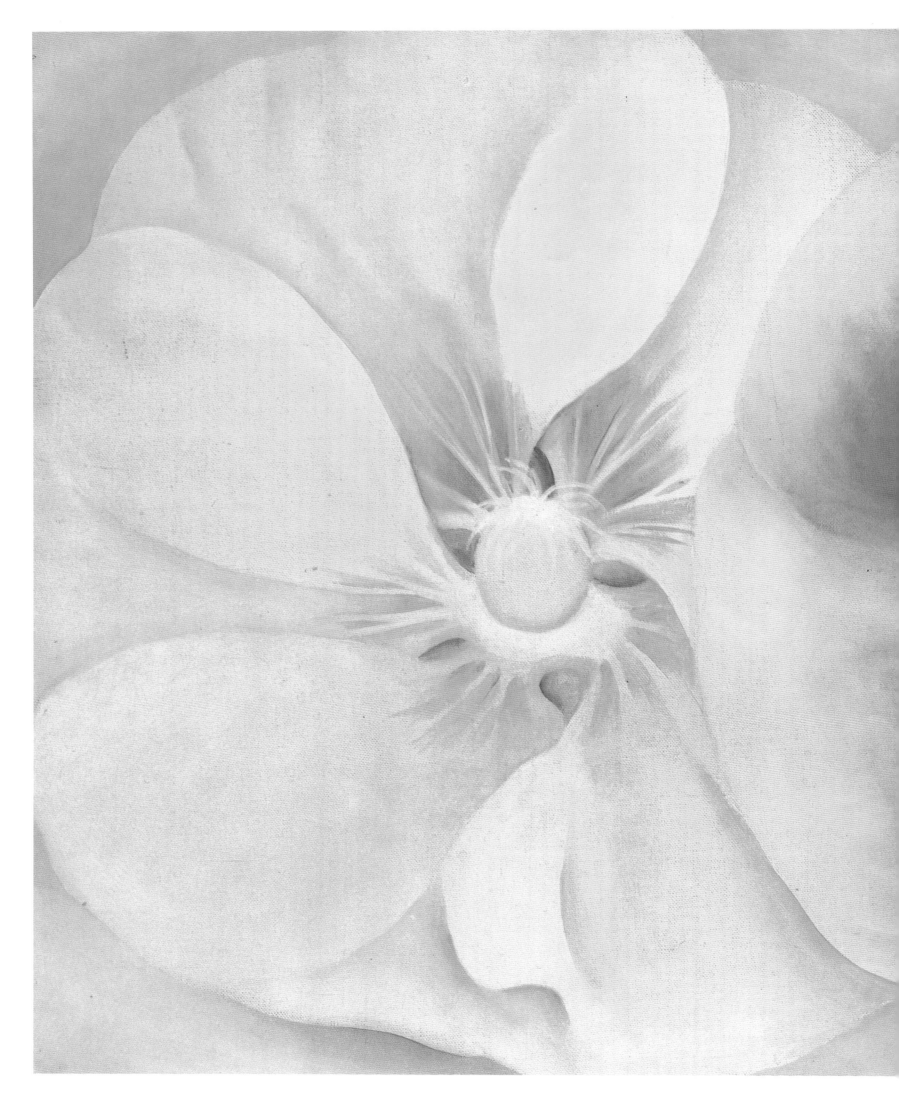

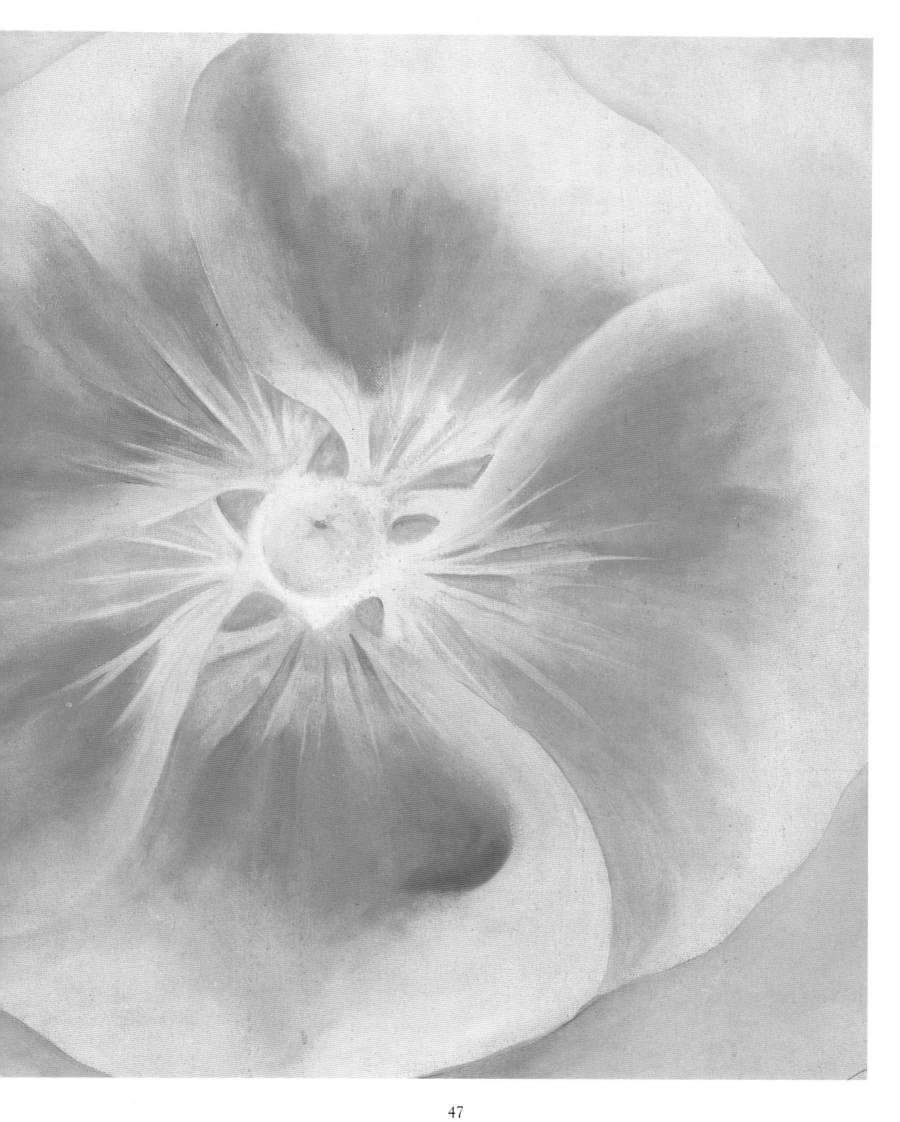

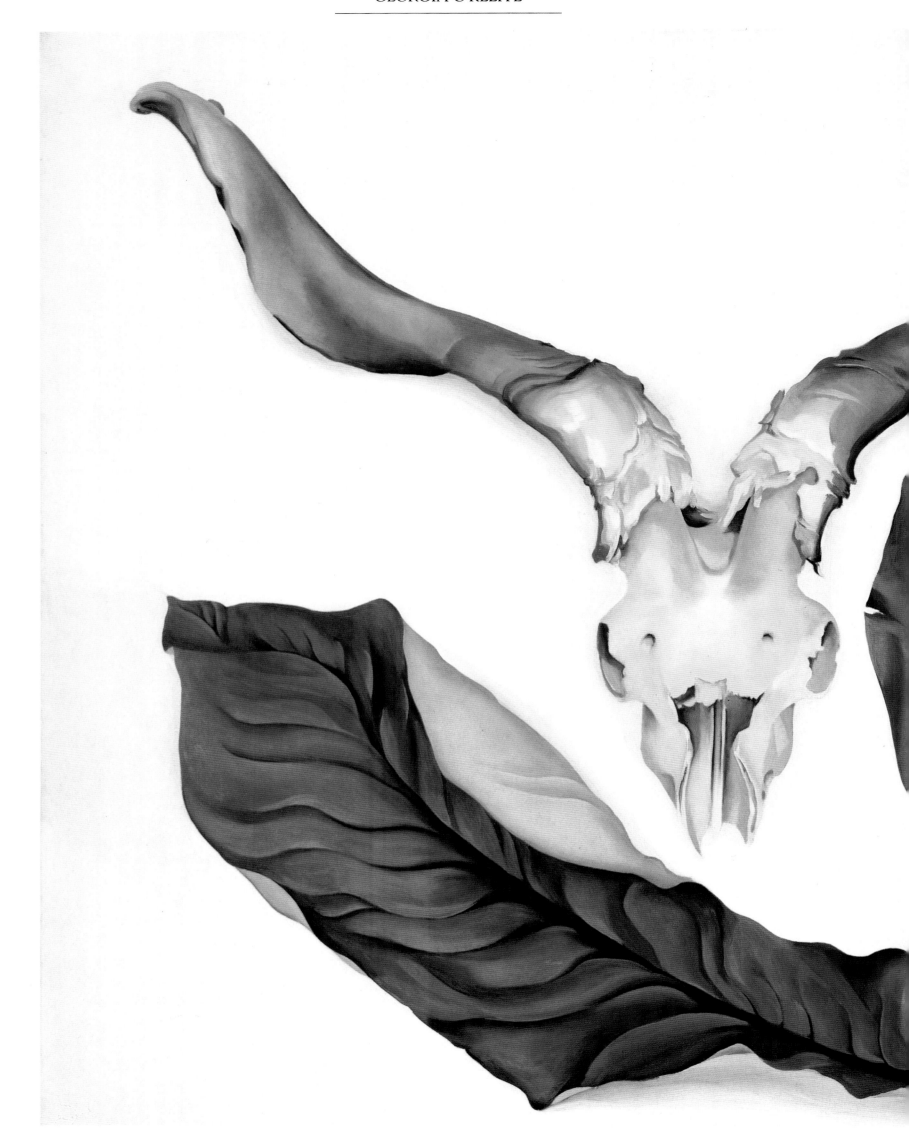

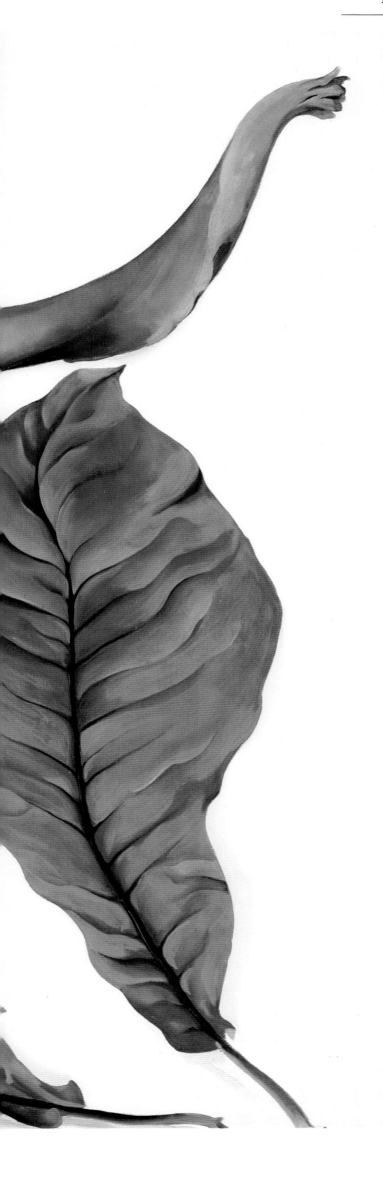

Ram's Skull with Brown Leaves
1936, oil on canvas, 30×36 in.
Gift of Mr. and Mrs. S. Marshall,
Roswell Museum, Roswell, NM

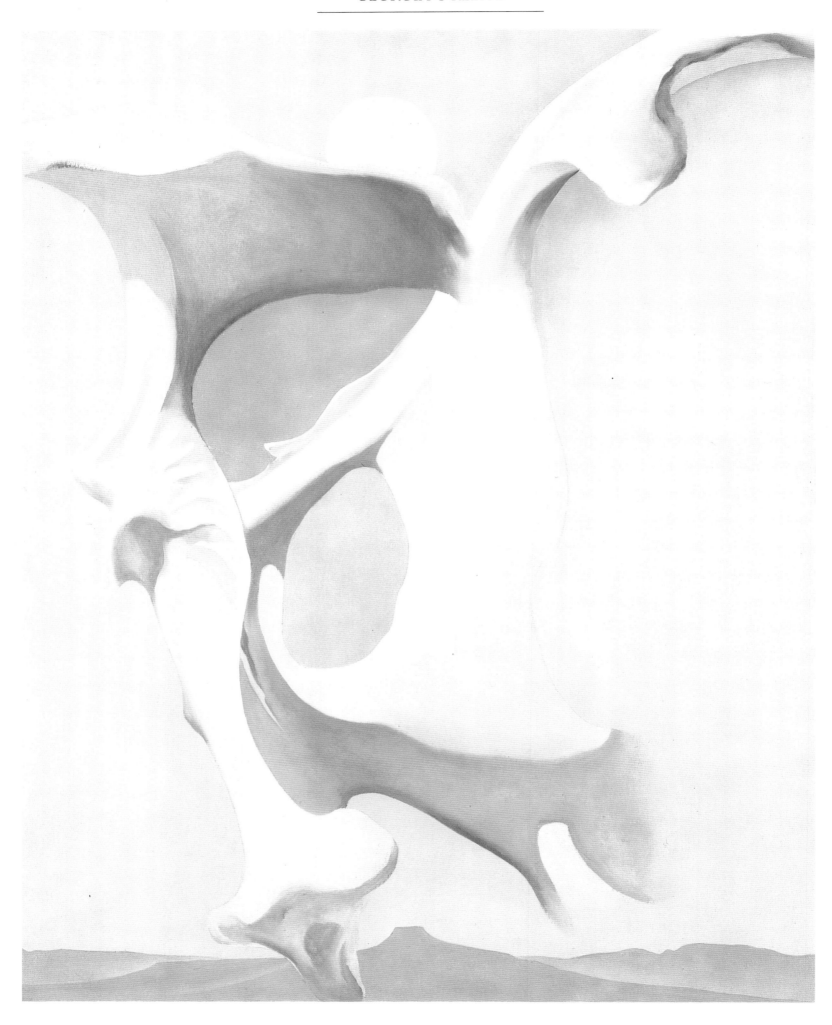

Pelvis with Moon
1943, oil on canvas, 30×24 in.
Collection of the Norton Gallery of Art,
West Palm Beach, FL

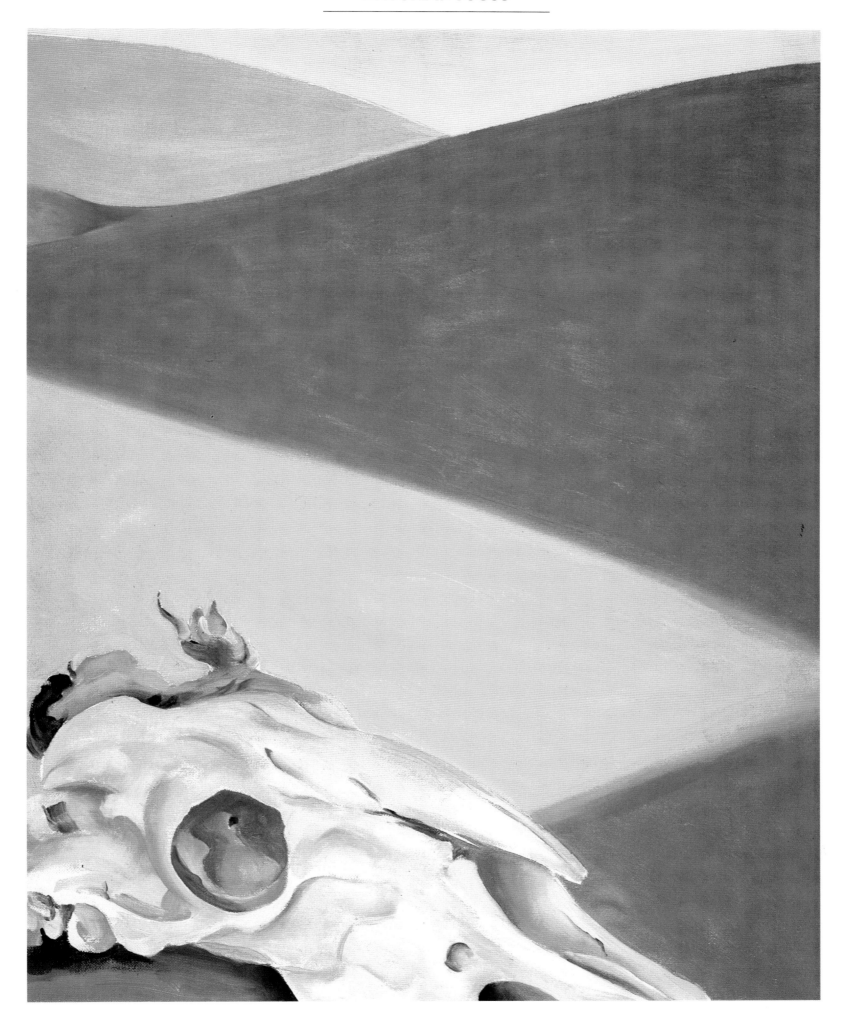

Goat's Head
1957, oil on canvas, 20×16 in.
Gift of the Estate of Tom Slick,
Marion Koogler McNay Art Museum,
San Antonio, TX
(1973.34)

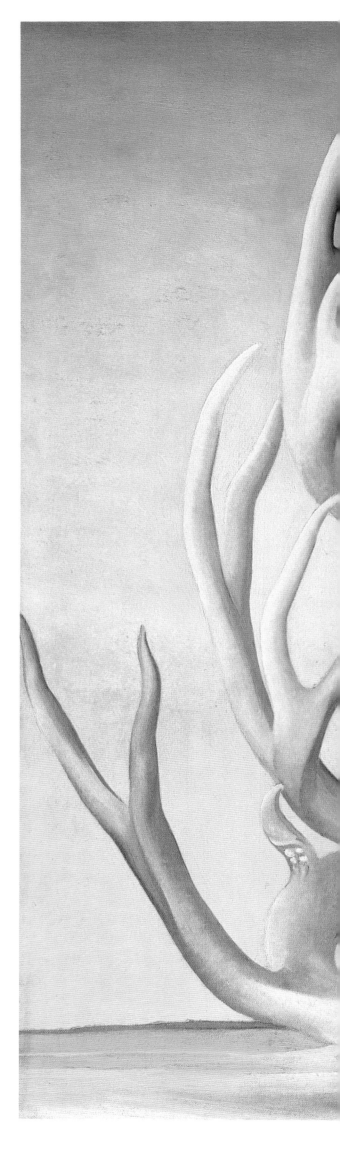

From the Faraway Nearby
1937, oil on canvas, 36×40⅛ in.
The Alfred Stieglitz Collection, 1959,
The Metropolitan Museum of Art, New York, NY
(59.204.2)

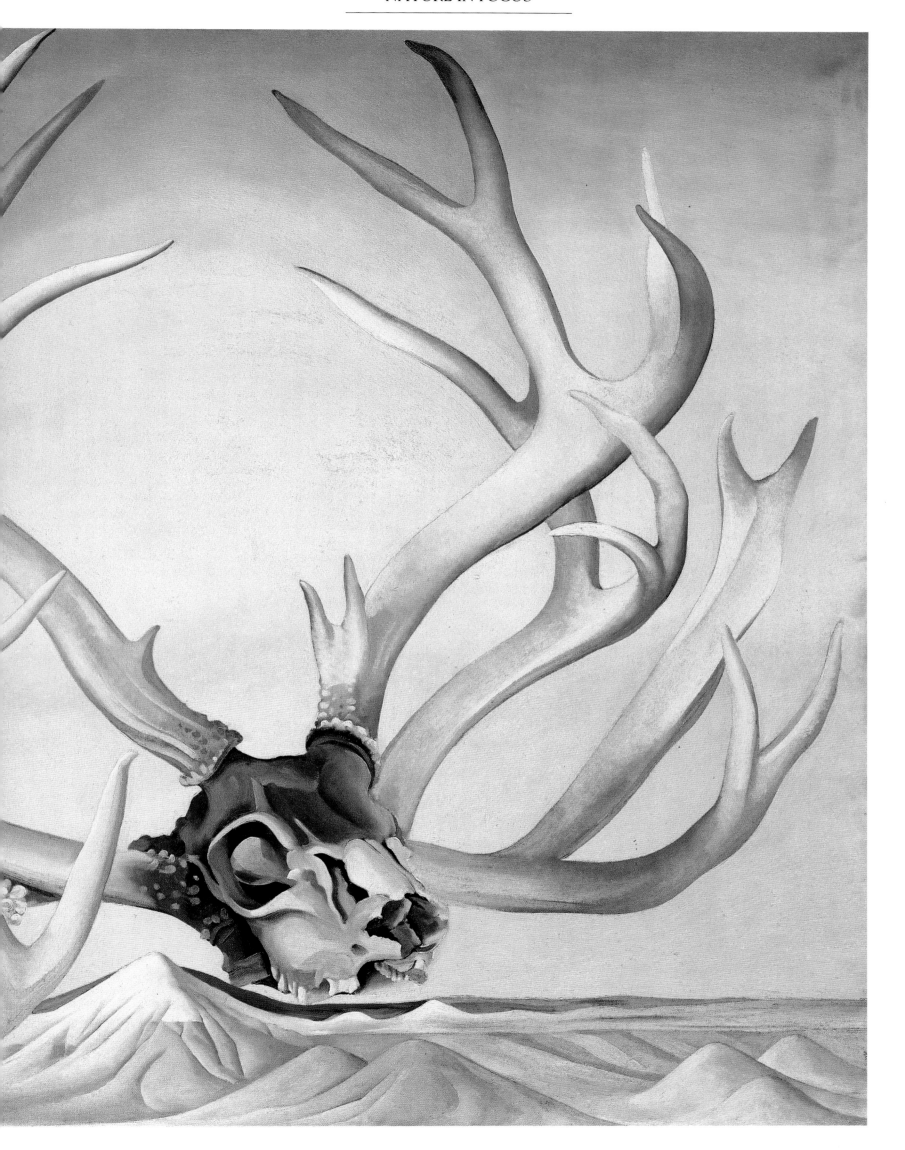

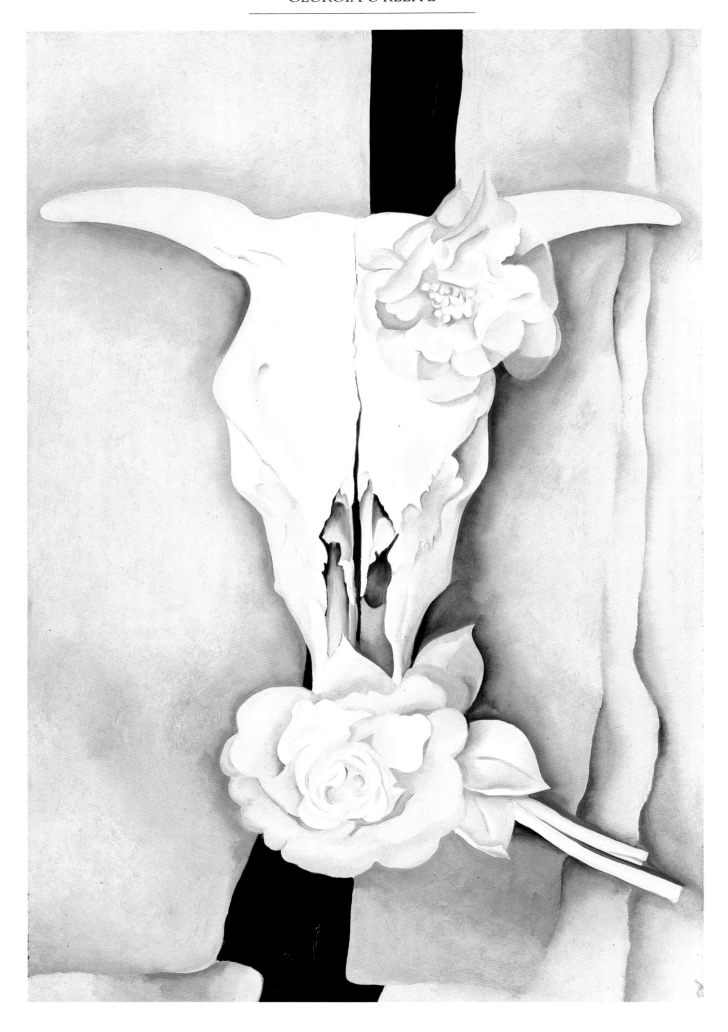

Skull with Calico Roses
1931, oil on canvas, 35.8×24 in.
Gift of Georgia O'Keeffe, 1947,
The Art Institute of Chicago, IL

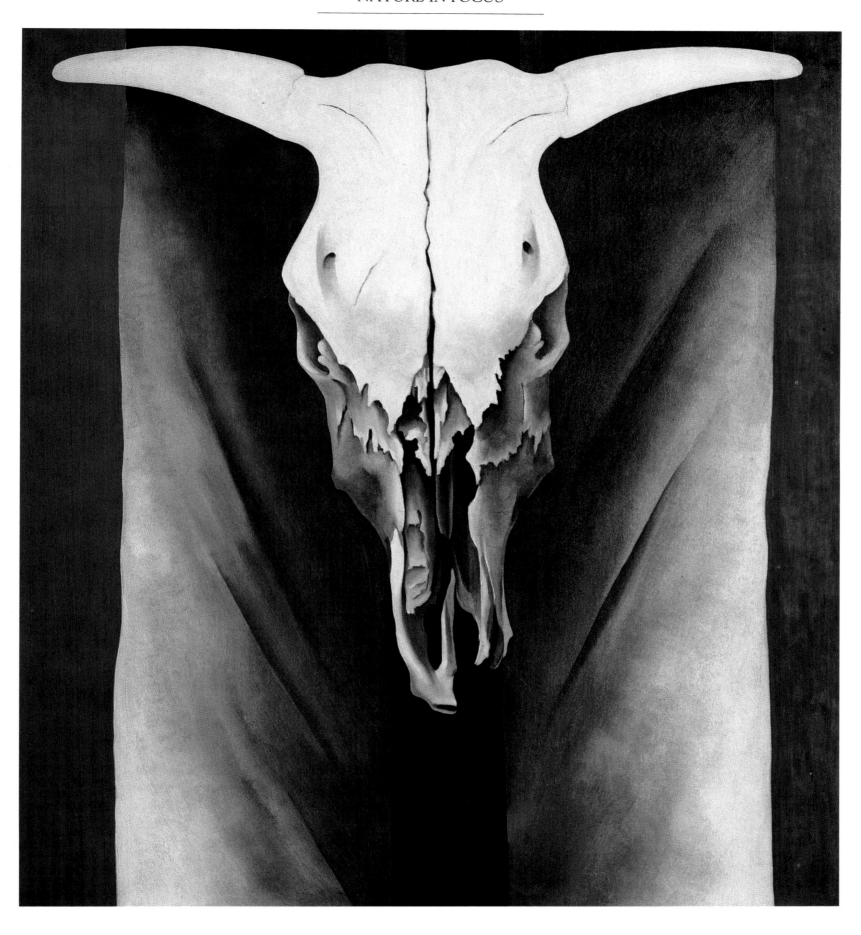

Cow's Skull: Red, White, and Blue
1931, oil on canvas, 39⅞×35⅞ in.
The Alfred Stieglitz Collection, 1952,
The Metropolitan Museum of Art, New York, NY
(52.203)

Overleaf:
Pelvis with the Distance
1943, oil on canvas, 23⅞×29¾ in.
Gift of Anne Marmon Greenleaf in memory of
Caroline Marmon Fesler,
Indianapolis Musem of Art, Indianapolis, IN
(77.229)

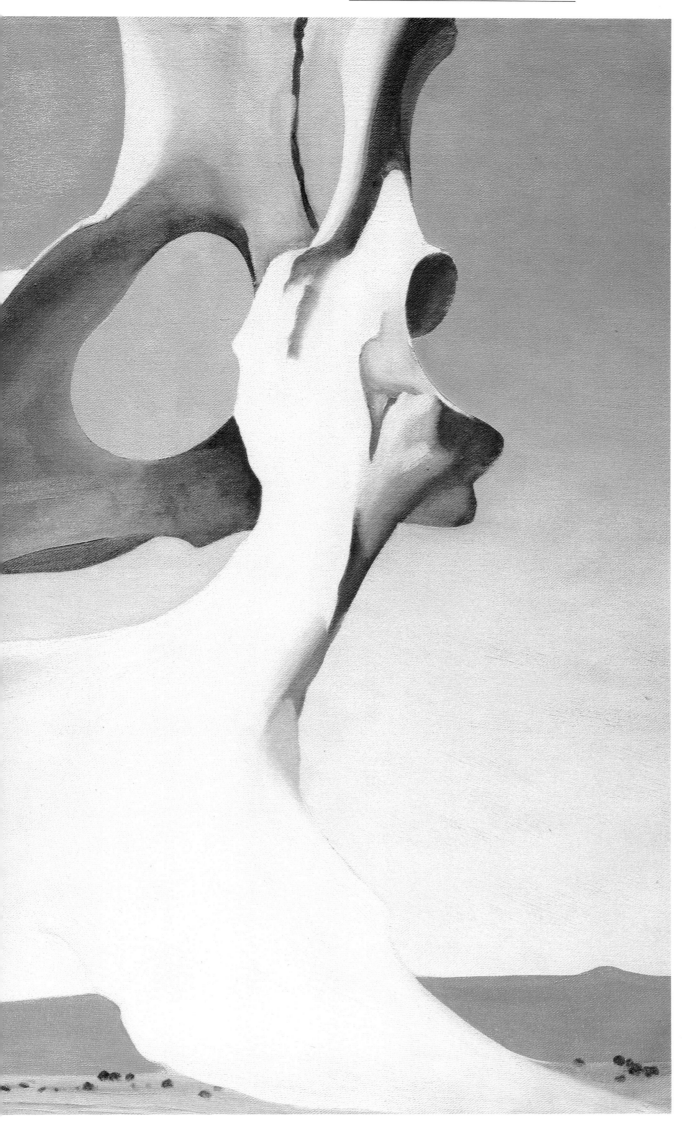

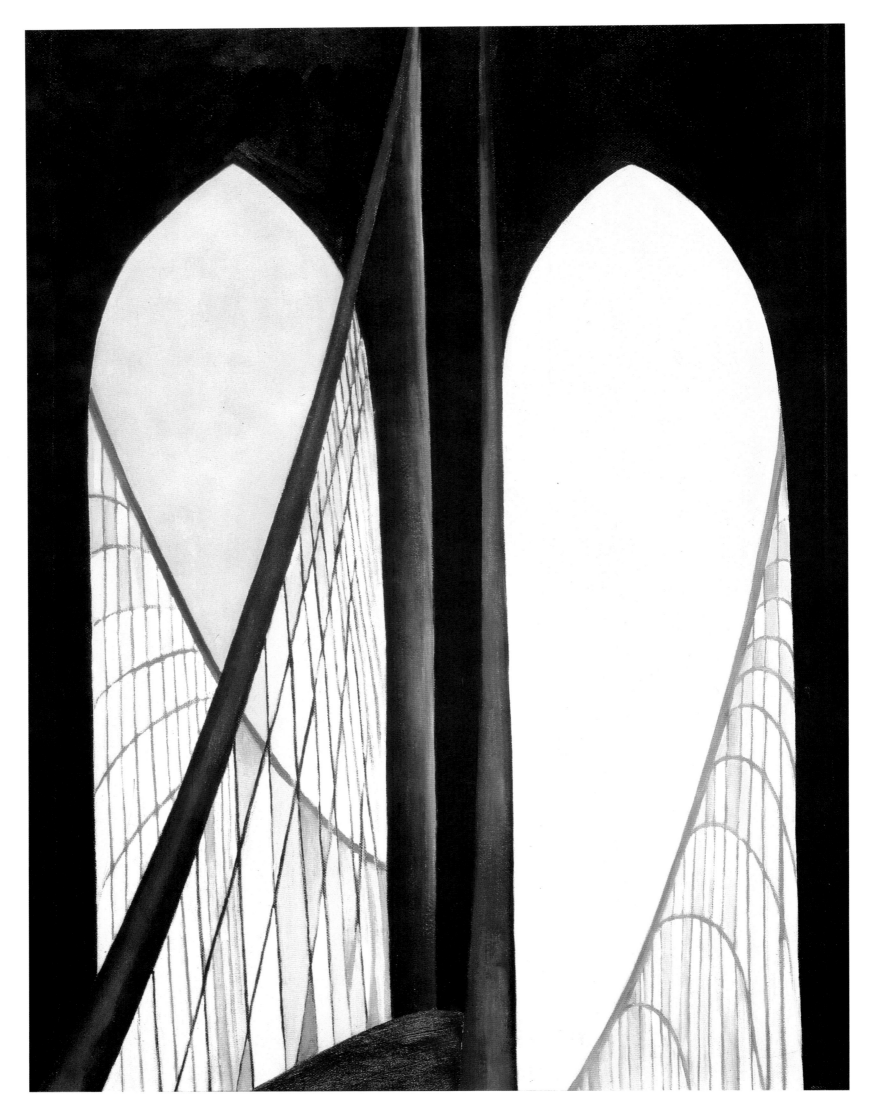

PLACES

Pictures of the landscape, like those of flowers, go back to the earliest art. Either as background or as the entire subject, the lay of the land provides a context for both mundane and spiritual drama. When American artists of the nineteenth century boldly claimed independence from European academicians, they did so by heroicising the great, newly explored, wild American landscape.

In the places she called home, New York City, Lake George, and New Mexico, Georgia O'Keeffe painted her surroundings. Sometimes her pictures were abstract, but often they were recognizable land- and cityscapes. O'Keeffe was powerfully affected by her surroundings. From the thirtieth floor of the Shelton Hotel in the City, where she and Stieglitz lived for a time, she looked at the river, and shadowy geometrical forms outside the window. Sometimes they appeared tinted with a soft, golden glow, sometimes with a harsher, reddish glare. And, although as time went on she almost never painted people, the skyscrapers she did paint are nearly anthropomorphic. Her *Radiator Building* has tremendous character and personality. *New York, Night* captures the city's liveliness and charm in an affectionate way.

Of Lake George, where she lived in the summers for about ten years, she said, "Very pretty. But, it wasn't made for me." Yet she carefully observed and painted the barn that could be seen from the kitchen window or the study where Stieglitz worked. A shanty was converted into a studio and one day, for fun, O'Keeffe painted it in what she called the low-toned and dismal colors her male colleagues used. When *My Shanty* was in an exhibition the men did, indeed, decide that she was finally learning how to paint.

The City and Lake George were home to O'Keeffe only in address. New Mexico became the locus of her spirit. As she wrote a friend, "I never feel at home in the East like I do out here – and finally feeling in the right place again – I feel like myself – and I like it."

In New Mexico, which O'Keeffe visited for the first time in 1929 and moved to permanently in 1949 after Stieglitz died and she had settled his estate, she eventually had two houses. One was an adobe house in the village of Abiquiu. The other was to the north of Abiquiu, surrounded by cliffs and hills. It had belonged to the Catholic church, and O'Keeffe had negotiated with the church, which was reluctant to part with the property, for ten years.

She went out to paint in a Model A Ford in which she had removed the back seat and, when she was working, turned the front one around. That gave her room for her canvas, and the back windows were high enough to provide plenty of light and a good view. In the heat of the day she sometimes crawled under the car for shade. At four o'clock the windows had to be closed to keep the bees out. During these excursions, and others when she and a friend might camp out overnight, she painted the haunting and prehistoric scenes.

She walked the desert and the hills and captured the earth and sky with deep affinity. The Pedernal was a flat-topped mesa that she painted repeatedly, constantly changing her perspective and her palette. "It is my private mountain," she explained. "God told me if I painted it enough, I could have it."

In these works, from the patio outside her adobe walls to the Pedernal in the distance, she seemed able to see eternity, and to find home there.

Brooklyn Bridge
1948, oil on masonite, 47$^{15}/_{16}$×35$^{7}/_{8}$ in.
Bequest of Mary Childs Draper,
The Brooklyn Museum, Brooklyn, NY

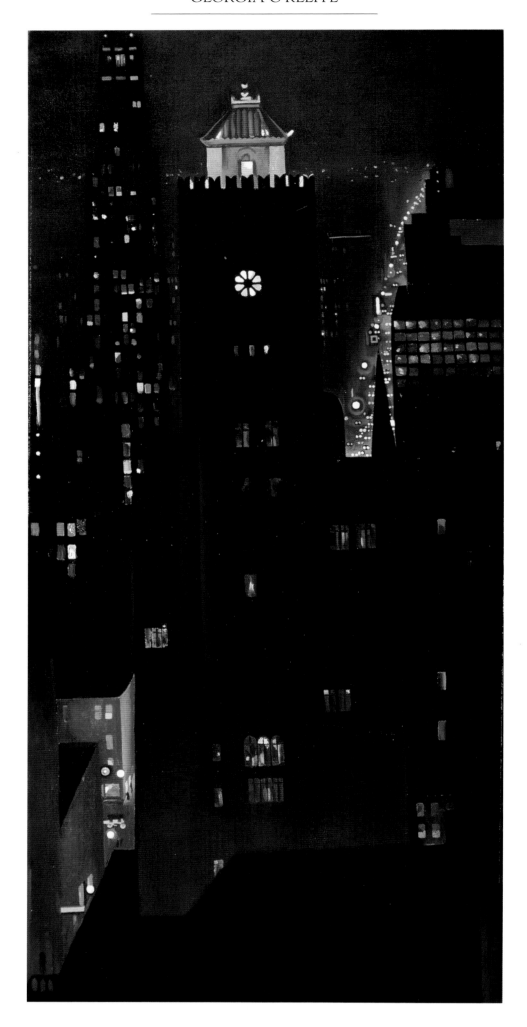

New York, Night
1928-1929, oil on canvas, 40⅛×19⅛ in.
Thomas C. Woods Memorial Collection, 1958,
Sheldon Memorial Art Gallery, University of
Nebraska, Lincoln, NB

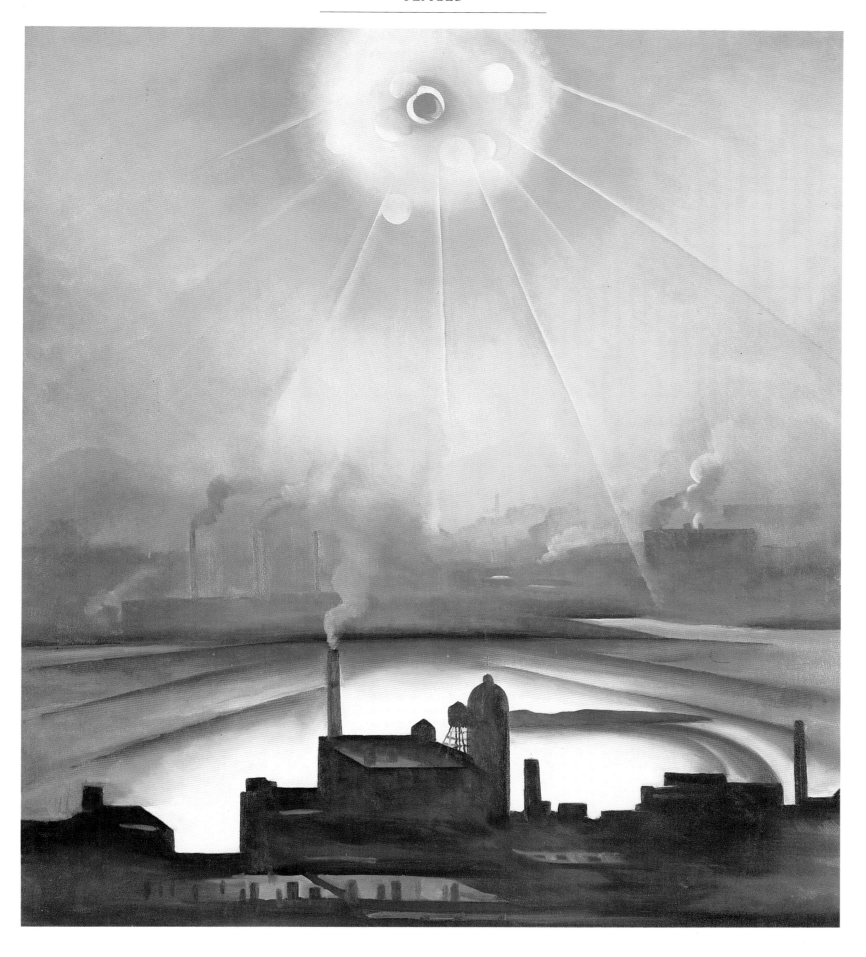

East River from the Shelton
1927-1928, oil on canvas, 25¹⁄₁₆×21¹⁵⁄₁₆ in.
Purchased by the Association for the Arts of the
New Jersey State Museum with a Gift from
Mary Lea Johnson,
New Jersey State Museum Collection, Trenton, NJ
(FA 1972.229)

Overleaf:
East River from the 30th Story
of the Shelton Hotel
1928, oil, 30×48 in.
Stephen Lawrence Fund,
New Britain Museum of American Art,
New Britain, CT

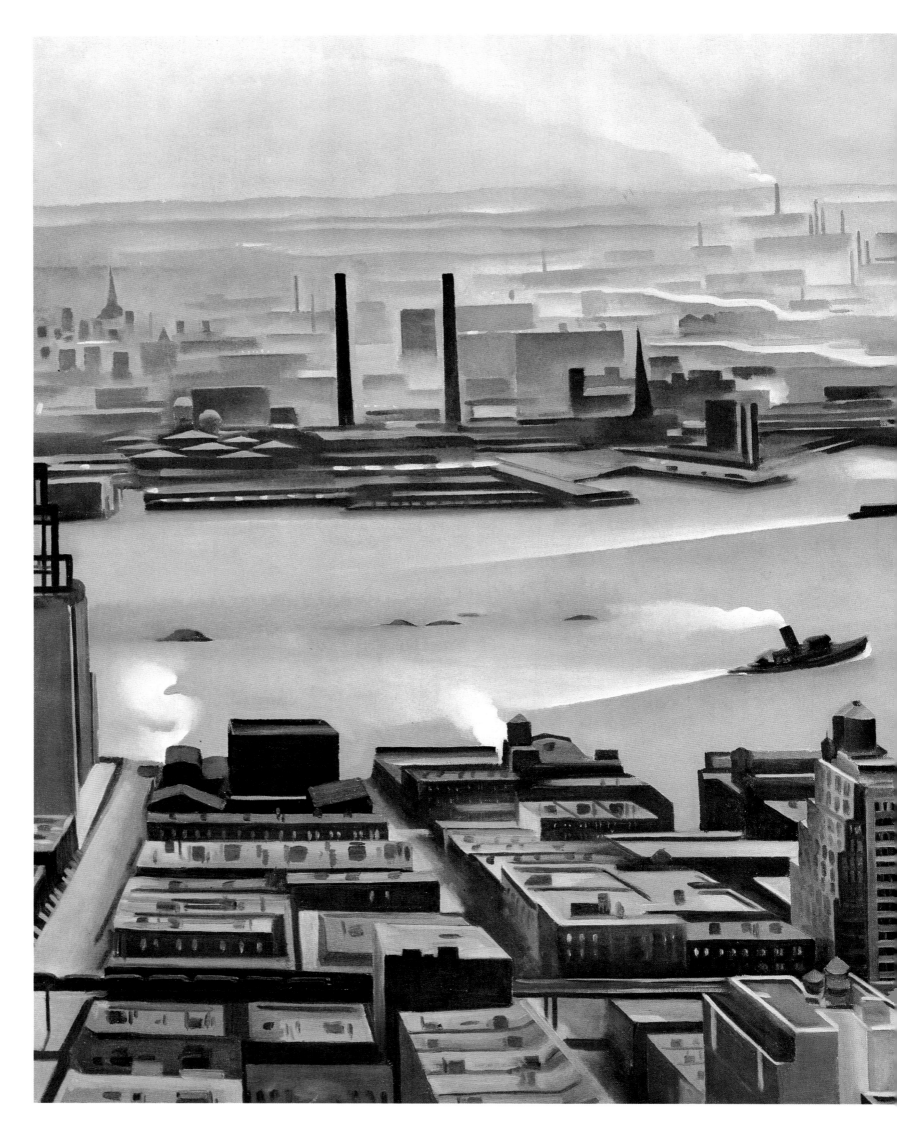

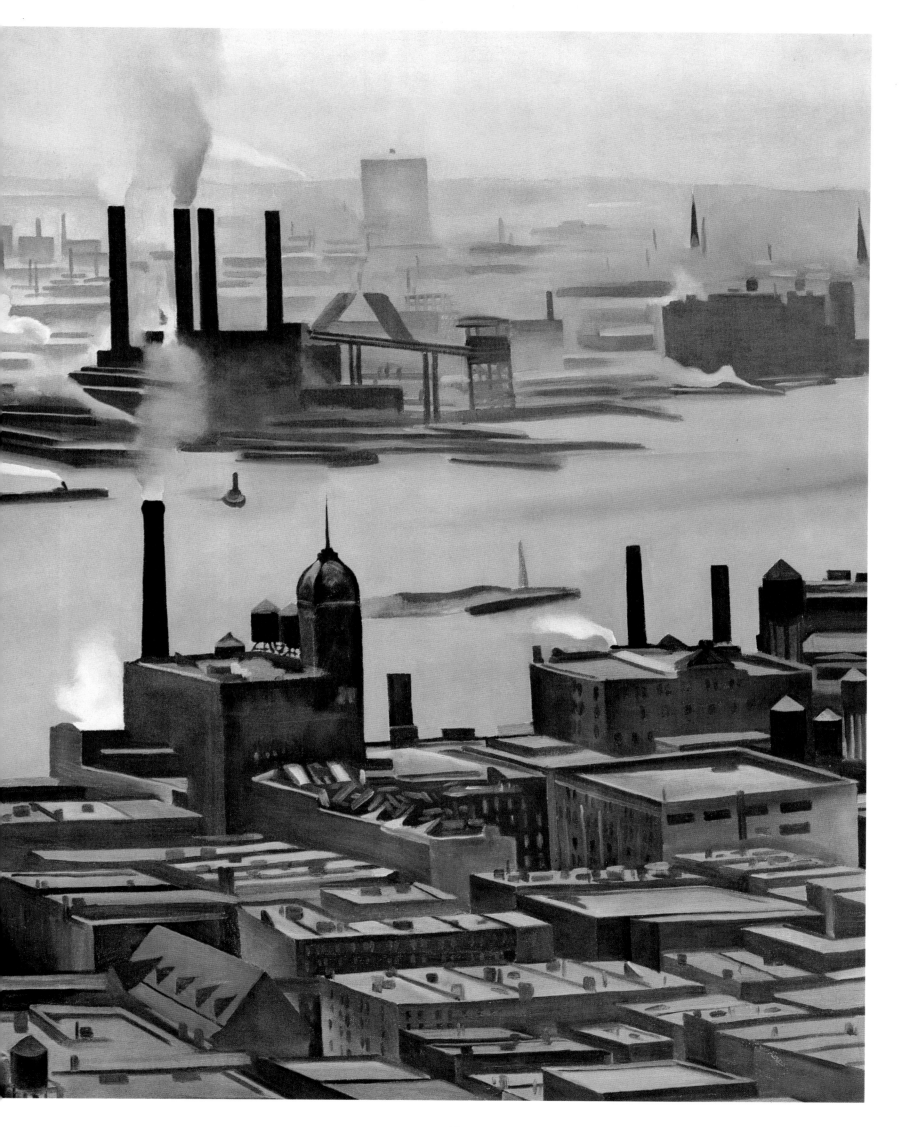

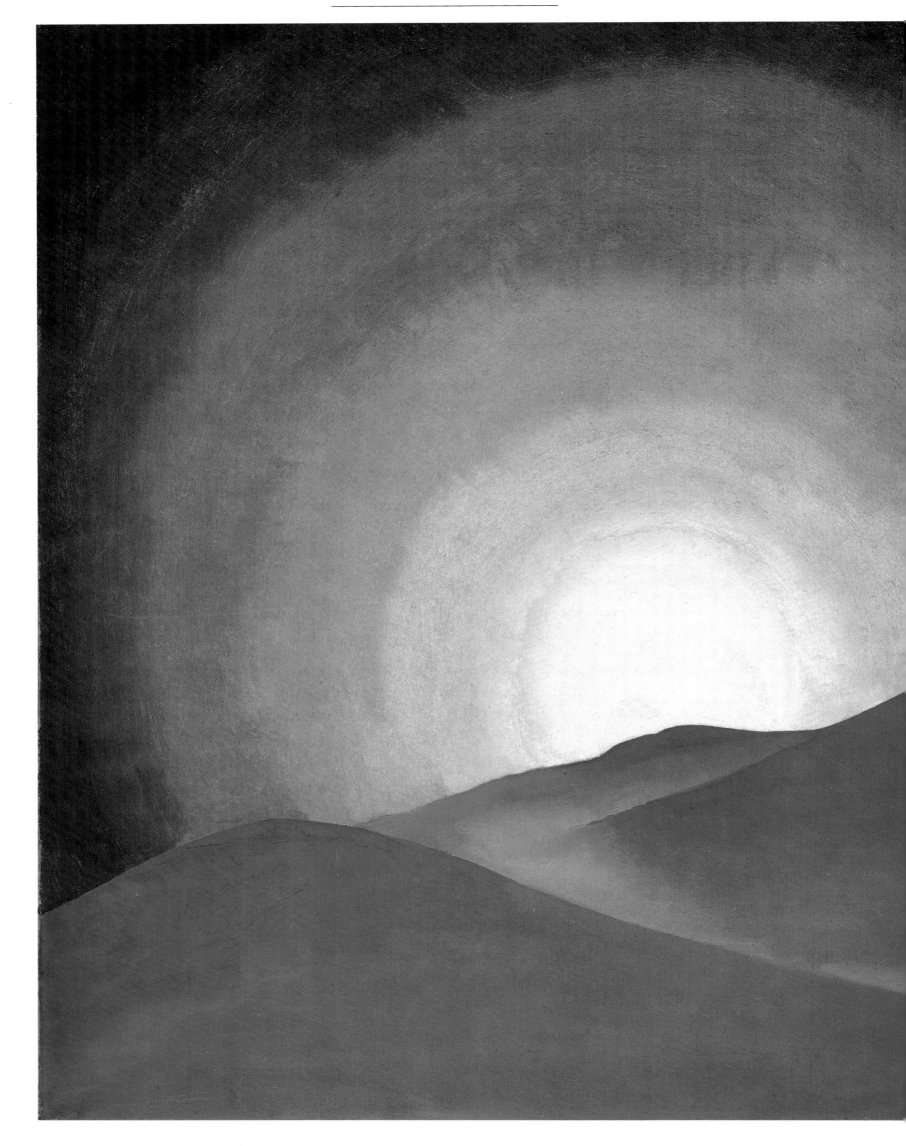

Red Hills, Lake George
1927, oil on canvas, 27×32 in.
Acquired 1945,
The Phillips Collection, Washington, DC

Overleaf:
Lake George Barns
1926, oil on canvas, 21⅛×32 in.
Gift of the T.B. Walker Foundation, 1954,
Walker Art Center, Minneapolis, MN

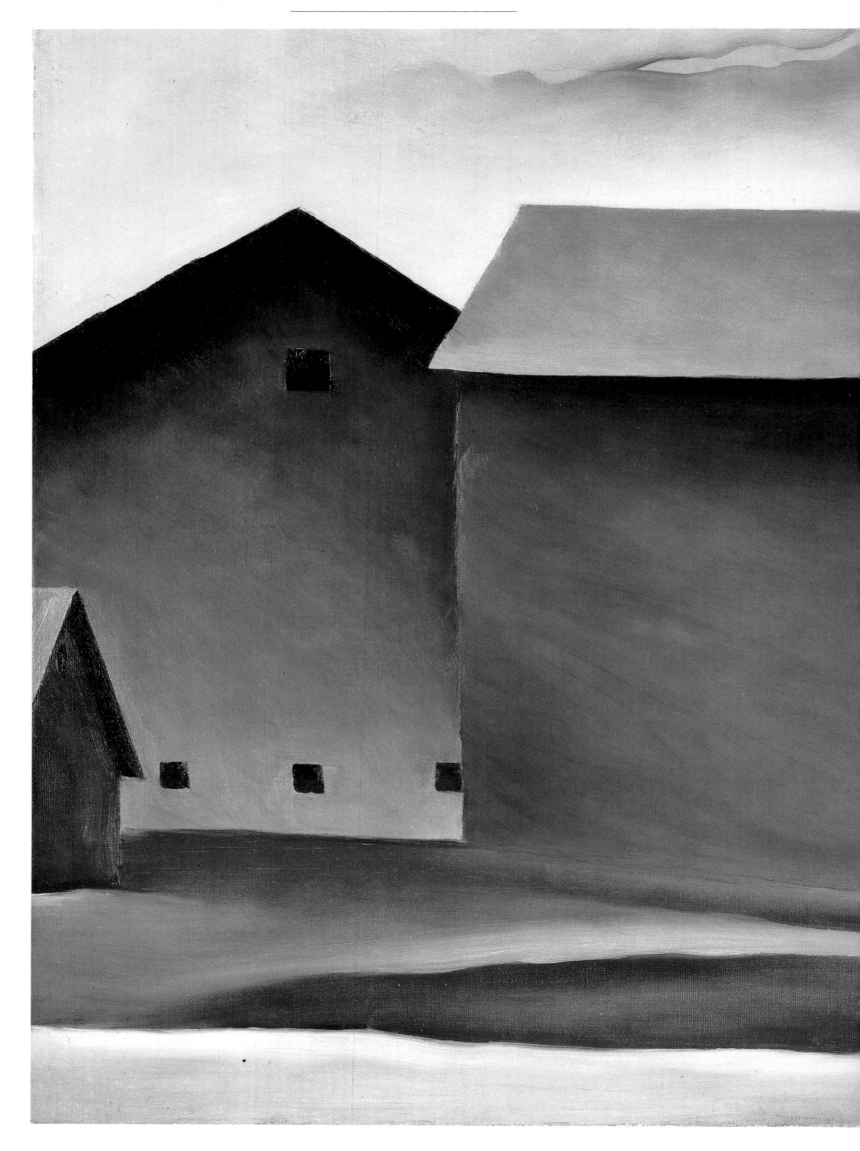

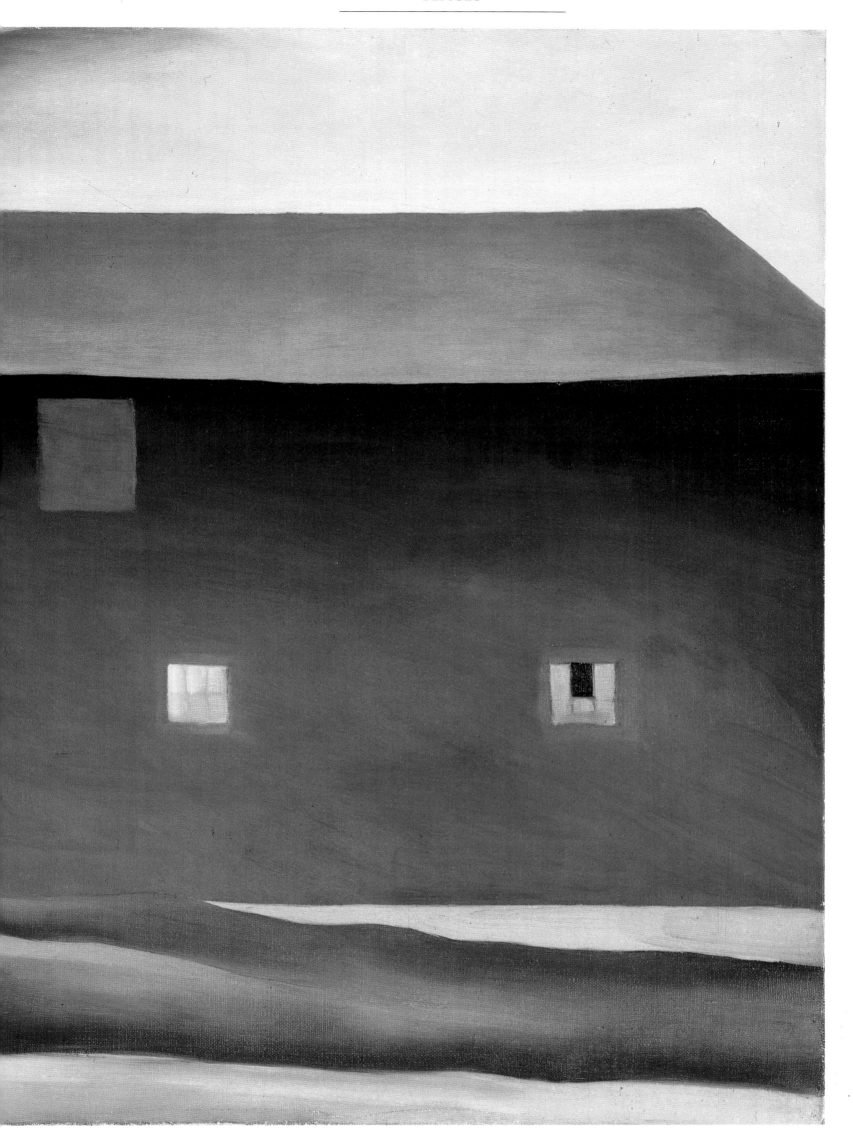

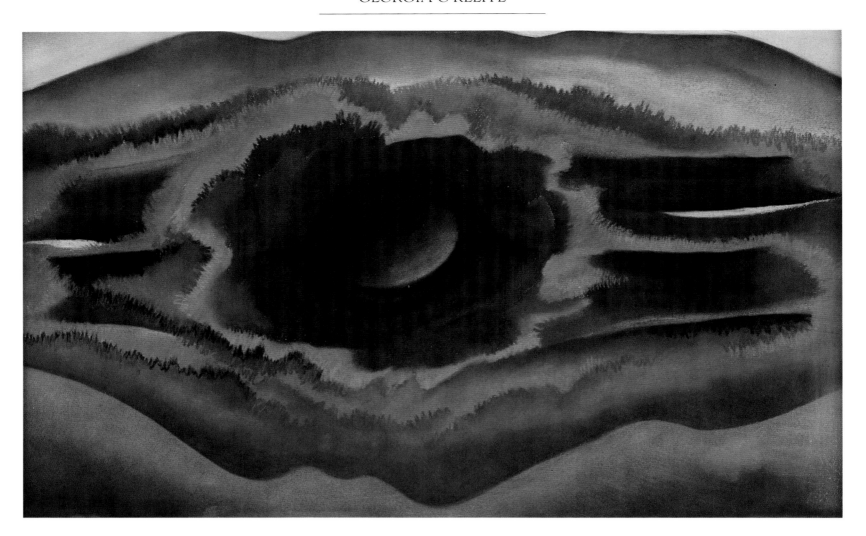

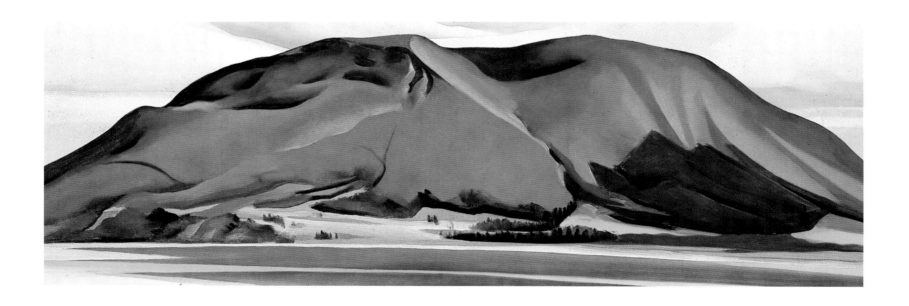

Top:
Pool in the Woods, Lake George
1922, pastel on paper, 17½×28 in.
Reynolda House Museum of American Art,
Winston-Salem, NC

Above:
Green Mountains – Canada
1932, oil on canvas, 12×36 in.
Gift of Georgia O'Keeffe to the
Alfred Stieglitz Collection,
The Art Institute of Chicago, IL
(1956.365)

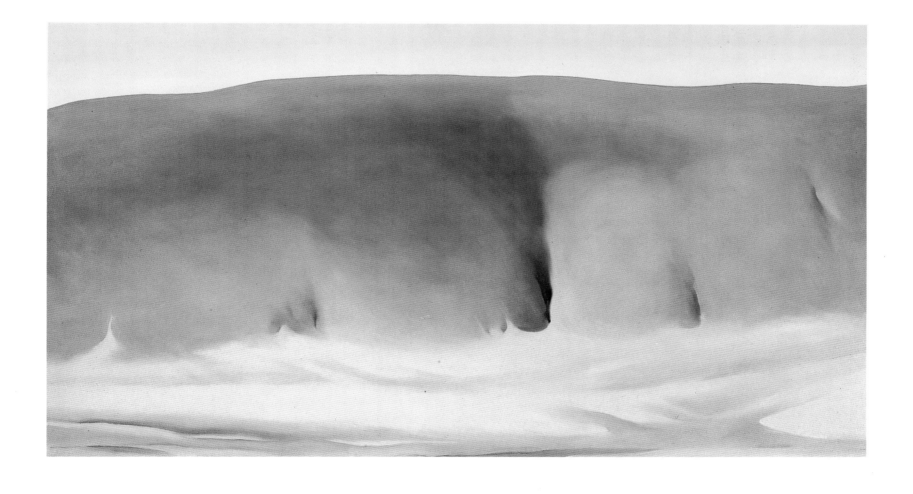

The Black Place
1943, oil on canvas, 19¾×35⅝ in.
Gift of Georgia O'Keeffe to the Alfred Stieglitz
Collection,
The Art Institute of Chicago, IL
(1969.834)

Overleaf:
My Shanty, Lake George
1922, oil on canvas, 20×27 in.
Acquired 1926,
The Phillips Collection, Washington, DC

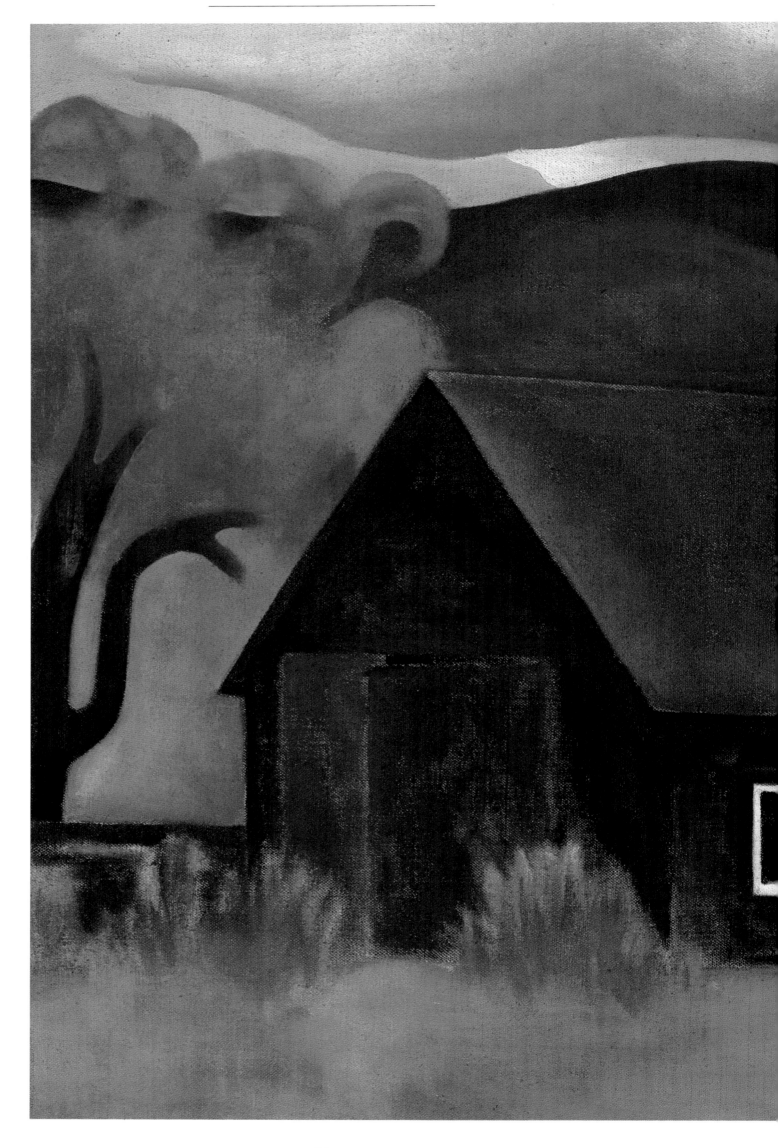

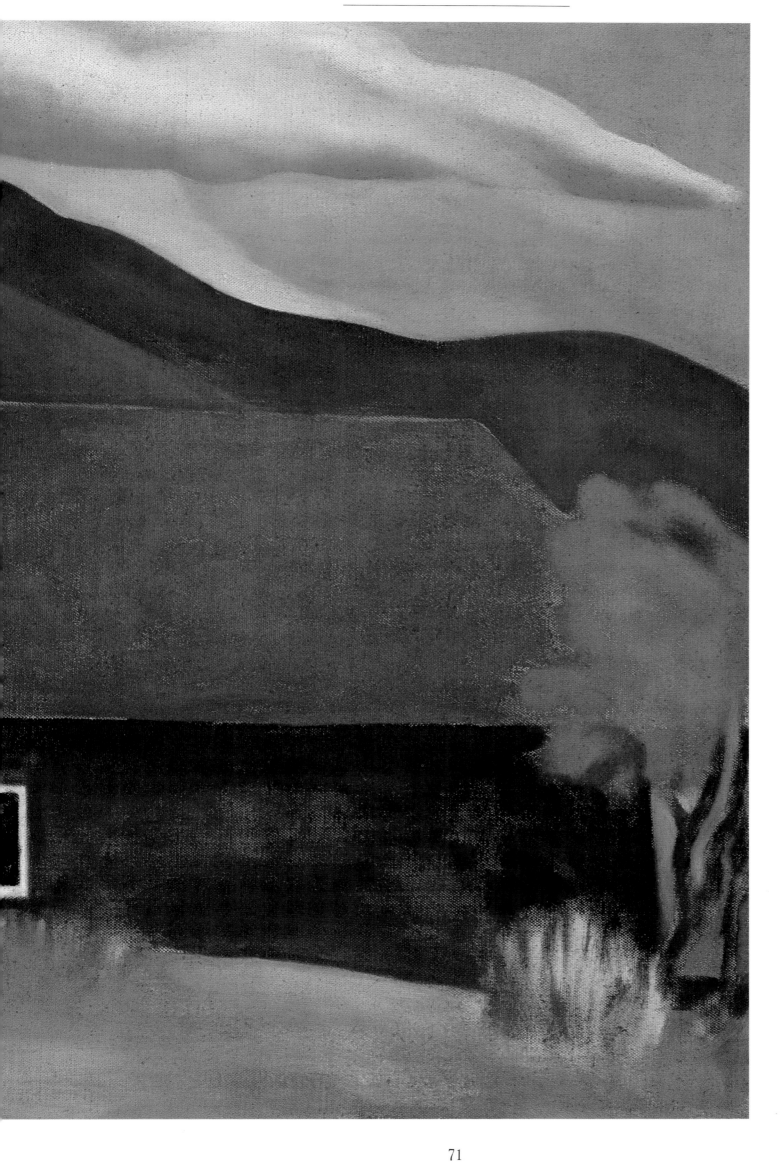

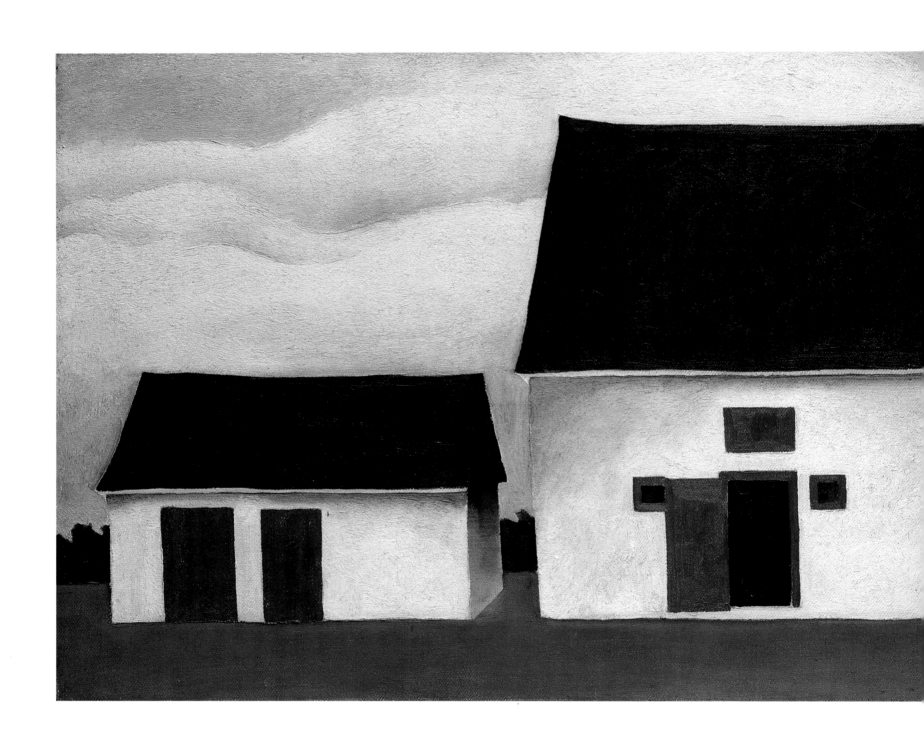

Stables
1932, oil on canvas, 12×32 in.
Gift of Robert H. Tannahill,
The Detroit Institute of Arts, MI
(45.454)

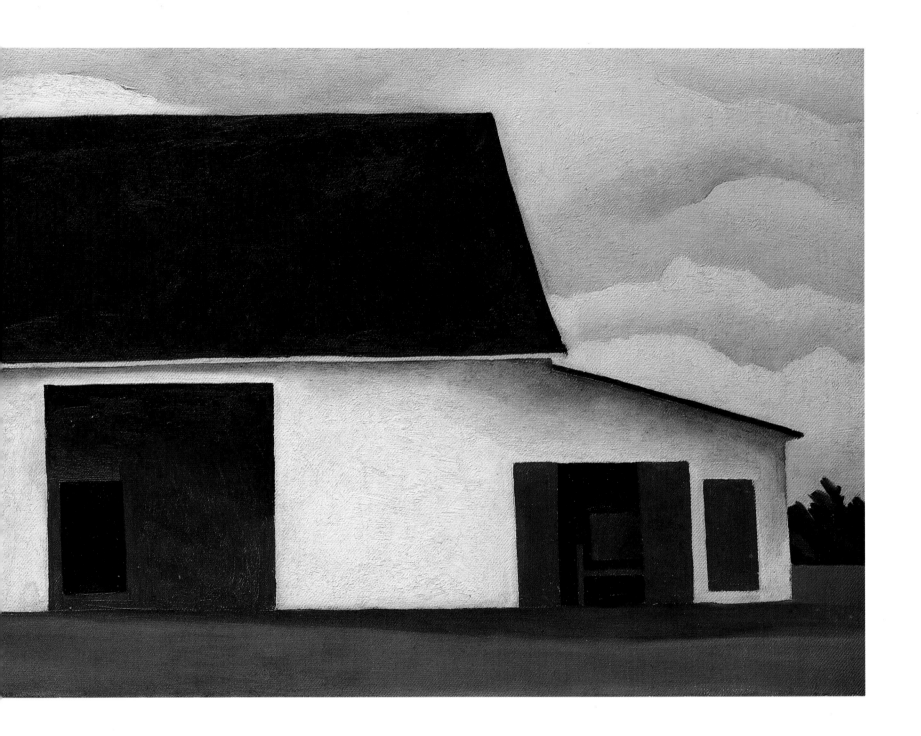

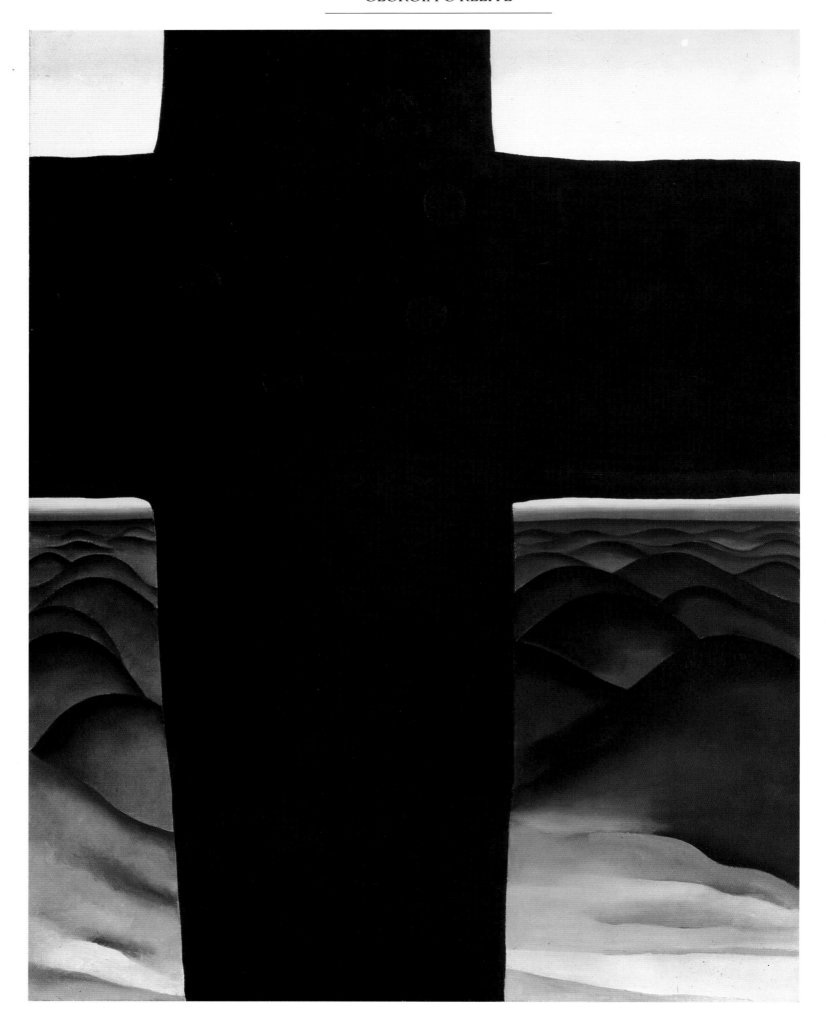

Black Cross, New Mexico
1929, oil on canvas, 39×30⅓ in.
The Art Institute Purchase Fund,
The Art Institute of Chicago, IL
(1943.95)

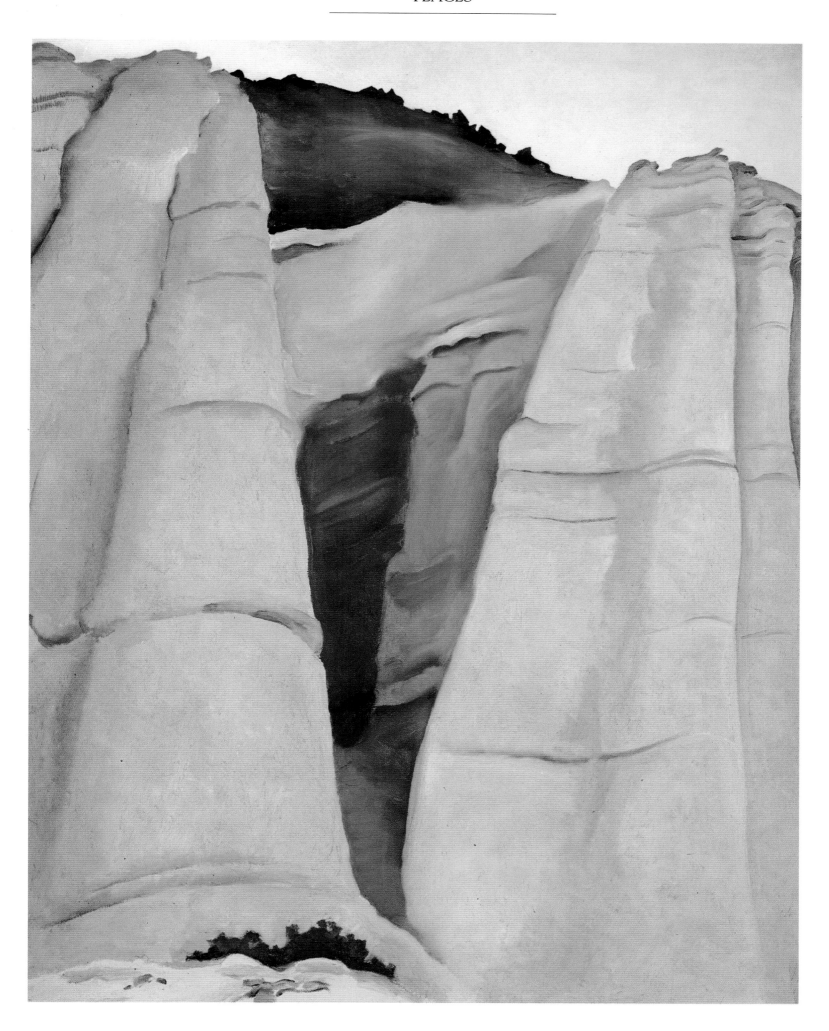

From the White Place
1940, oil on canvas, 30×24 in.
Acquired 1941,
The Phillips Collection, Washington, DC

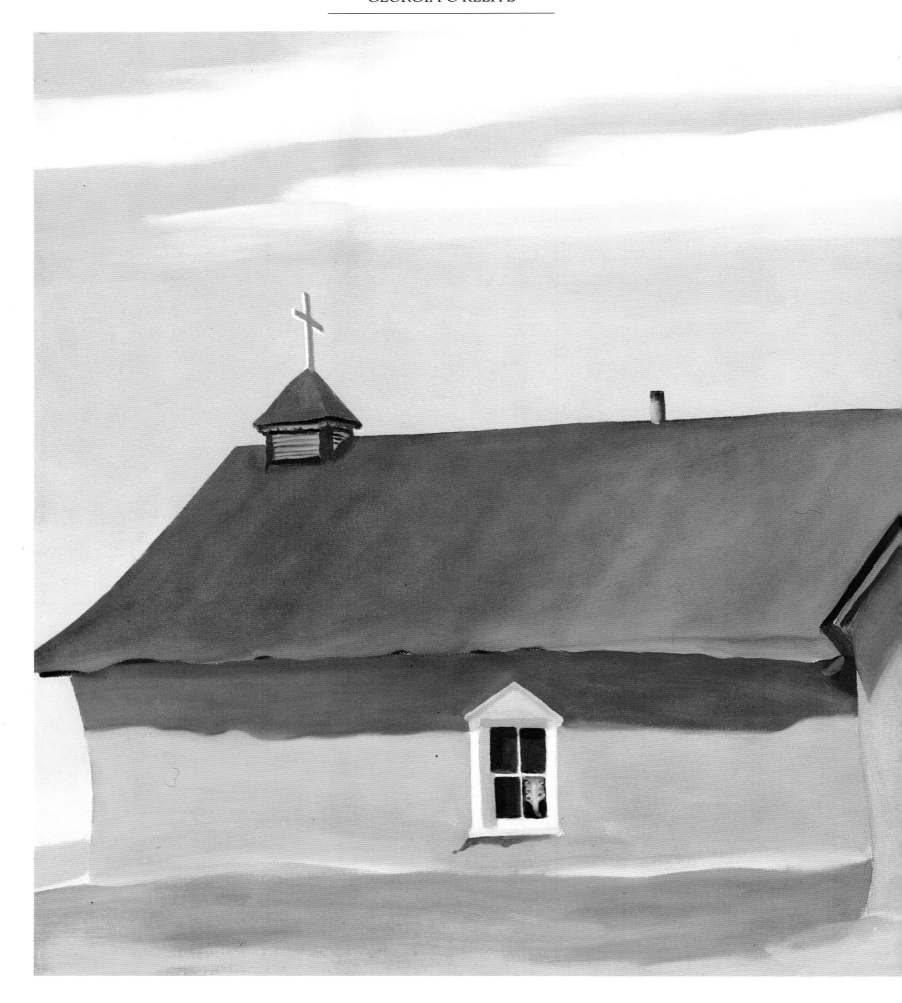

Cebolla Church
1945, oil on canvas, 20×36⅛ in.
Bequest of Robert F. Phifer in honor of
Dr. Joseph C. Sloane,
North Carolina Museum of Art, Raleigh, NC

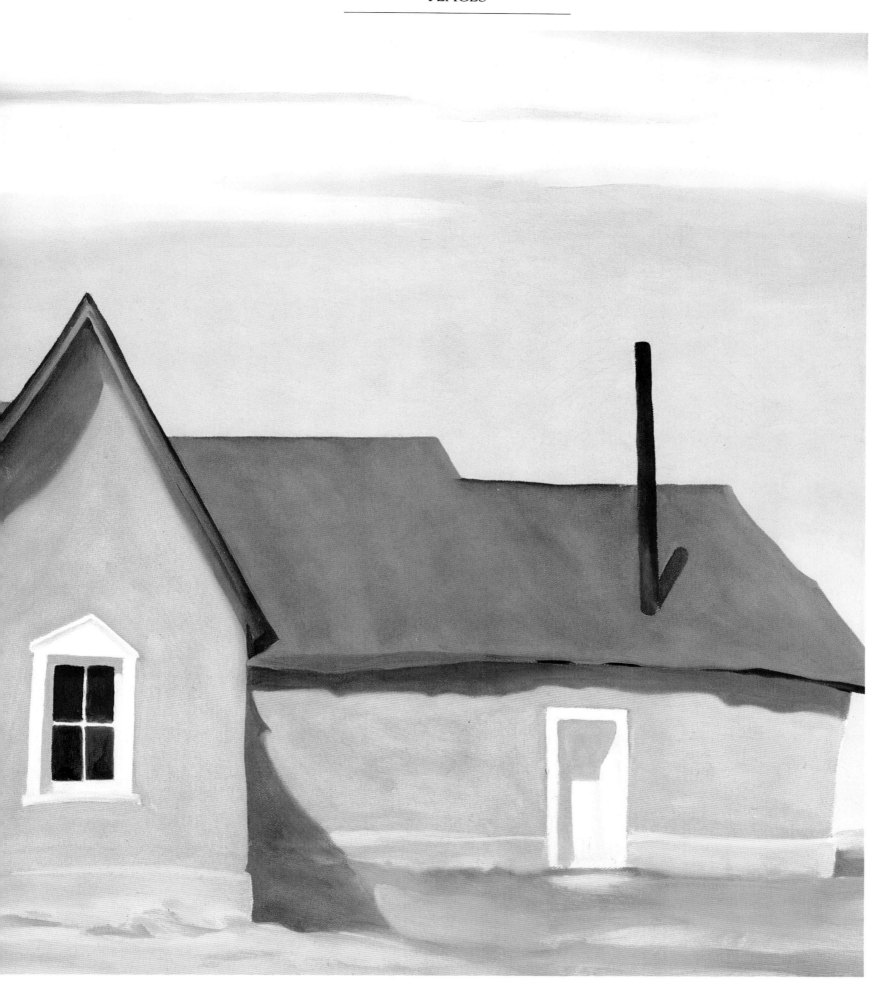

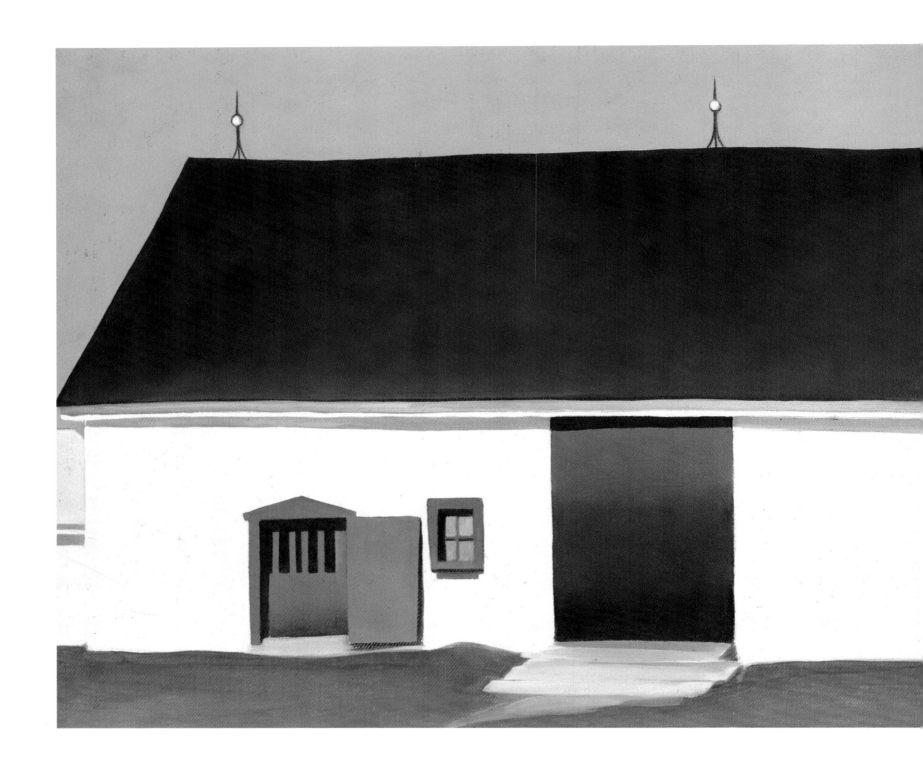

White Canadian Barn No. 2
1932, oil on canvas, 12×30 in.
The Alfred Stieglitz Collection,
The Metropolitan Museum of Art, New York, NY

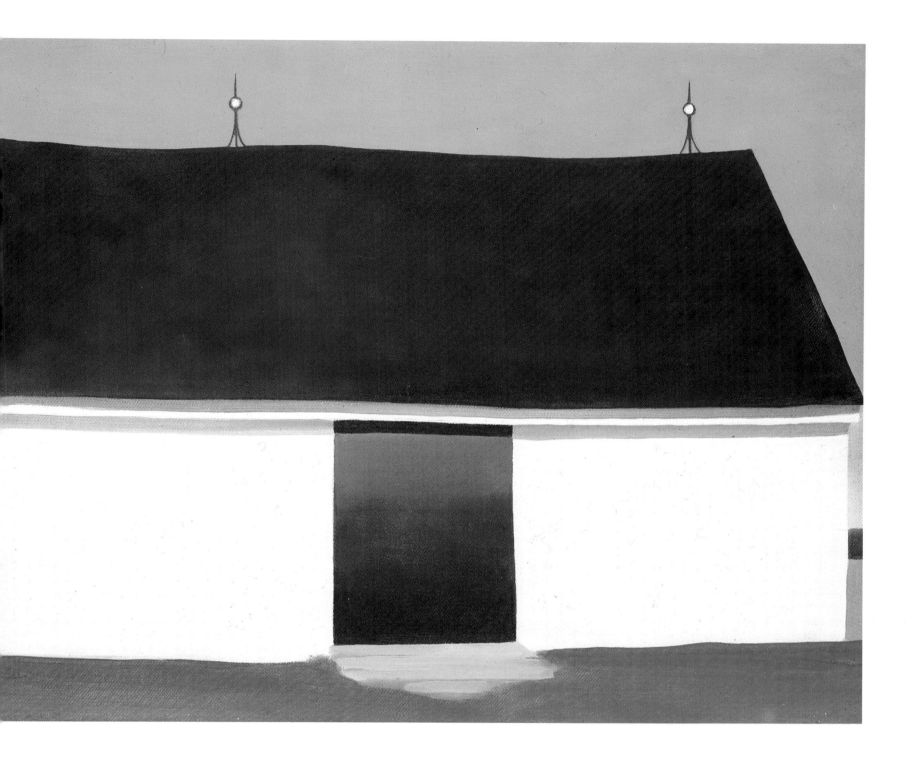

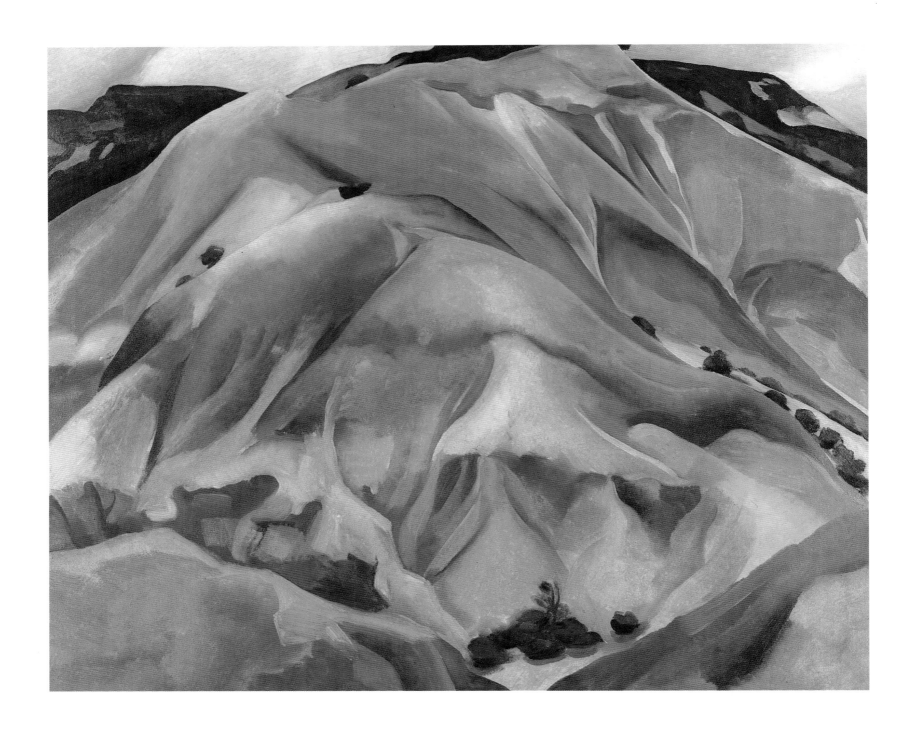

The Mountain, New Mexico
1931, oil on canvas, 30×36 in.
Purchased, Whitney Museum of American Art,
New York, NY
(32.14)

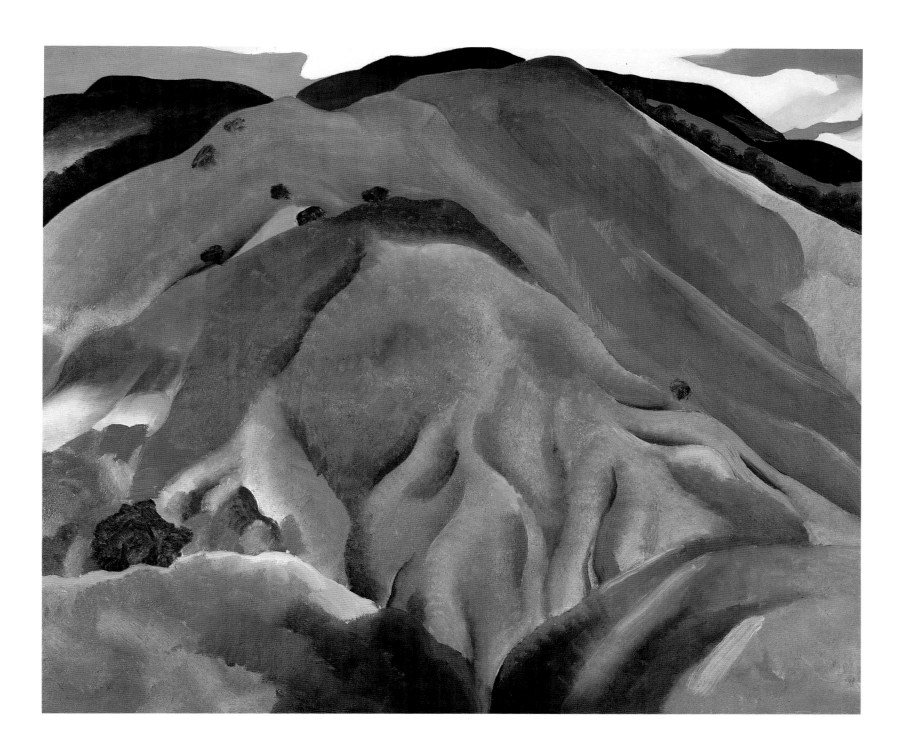

The Red Hills Beyond Abiquiu
1930, oil, 30×36 in.
Eiteljorg Museum of American Indian
and Western Art,
Indianapolis, IN

Overleaf:
Red Hills, Grey Sky
1935, oil on canvas, 14×20 in.
Courtesy of The Anschutz Collection

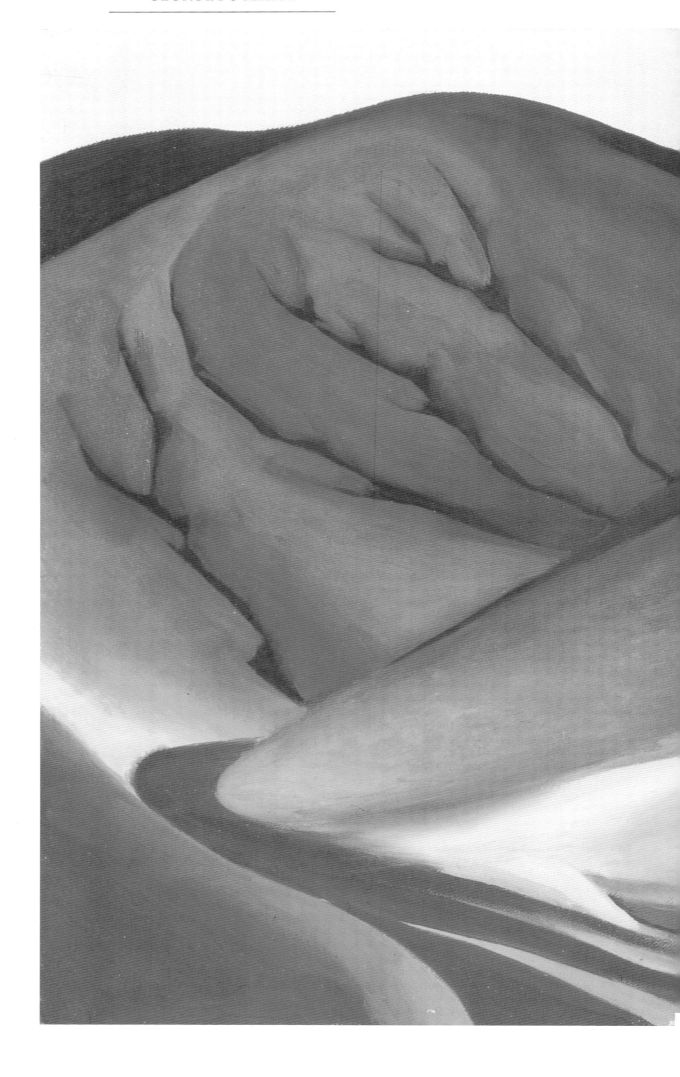

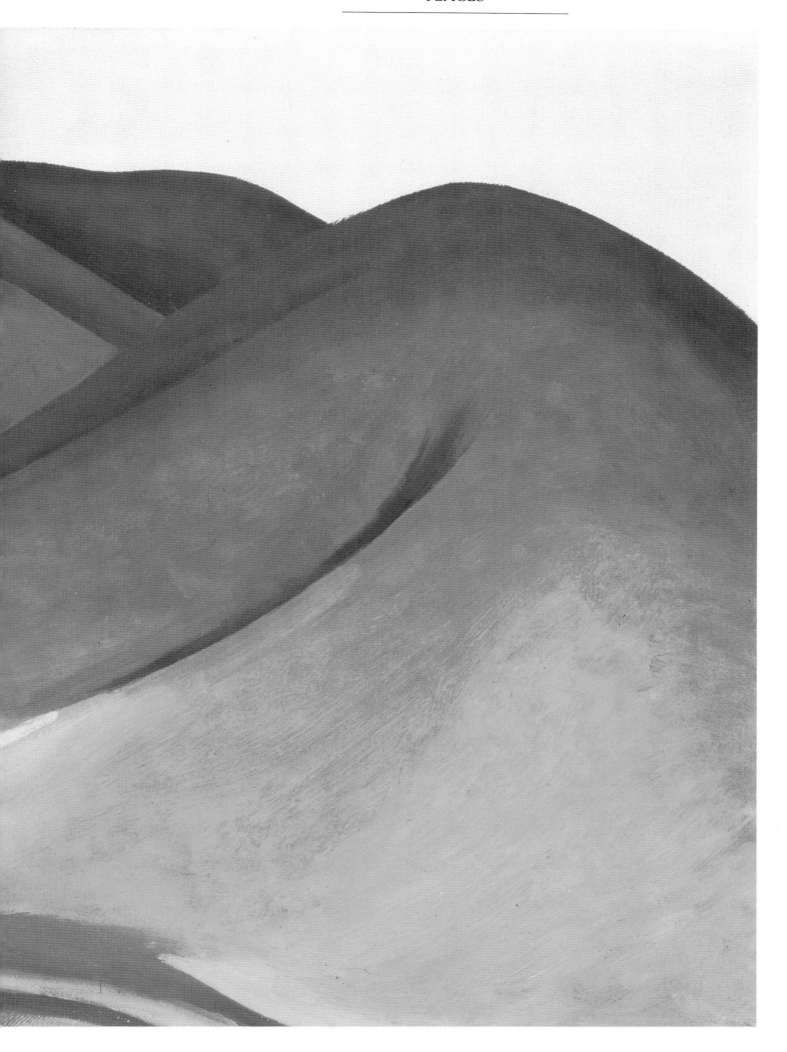

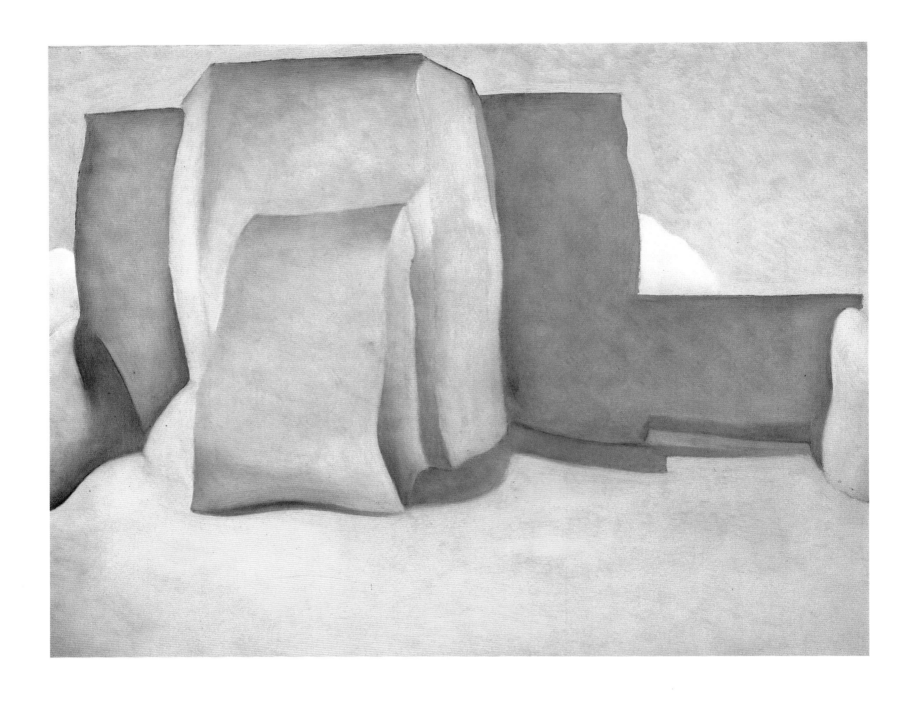

Ranchos Church No. 1
1929, oil on canvas, 18¾×24 in.
Norton Gallery of Art, West Palm Beach, FL

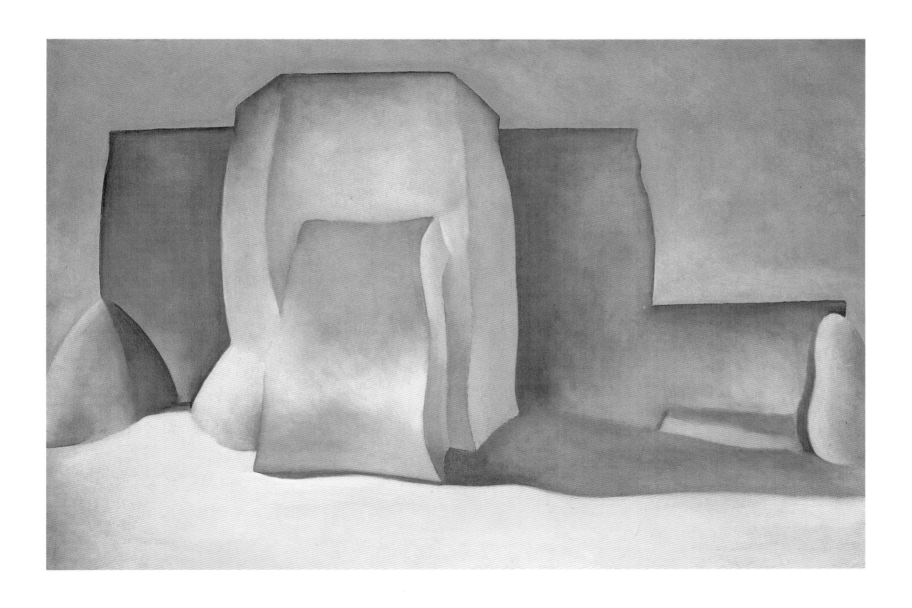

Ranchos Church
1929, oil on canvas, 24×36 in.
Acquired 1930
The Phillips Collection, Washington, DC

Overleaf:
The Gray Hills
1942, oil on canvas, 20×30 in.
Gift of Mr. and Mrs. James W. Fesler,
Indianapolis Museum of Art, Indianapolis, IN.

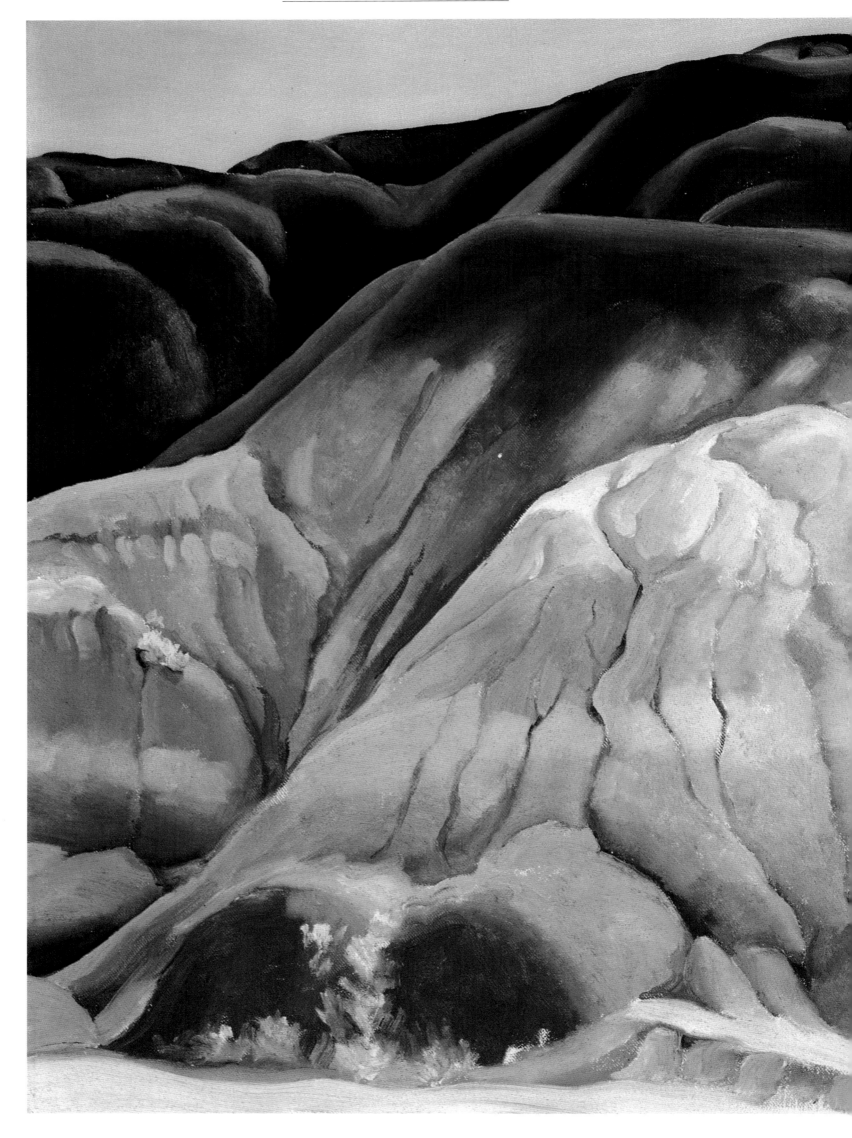

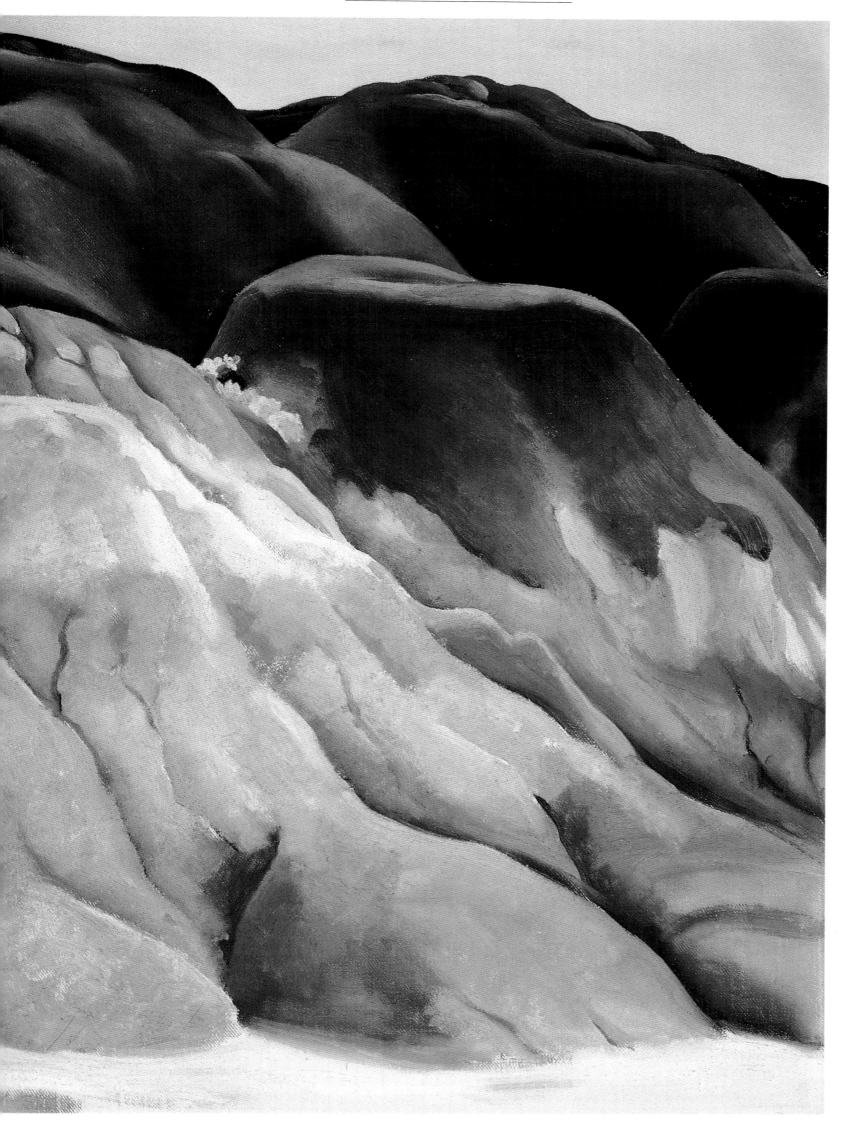

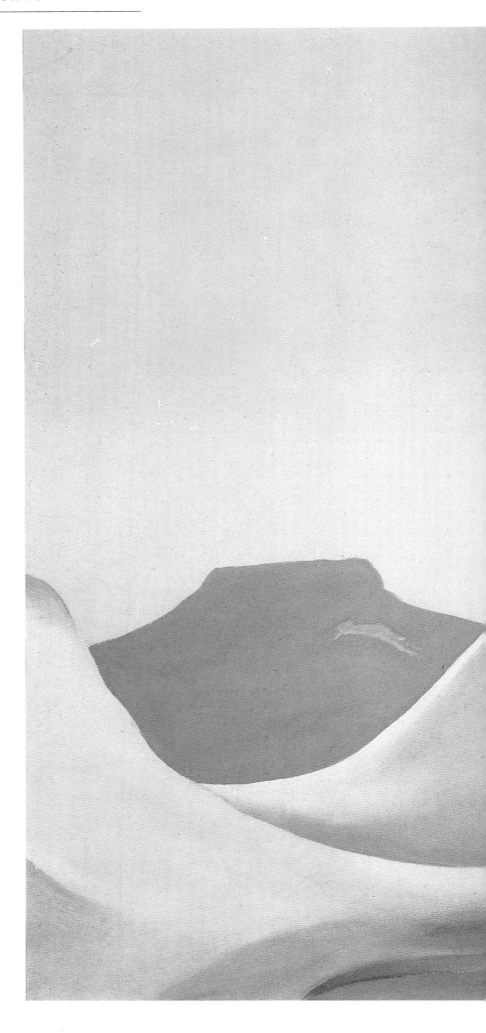

Pelvis with Pedernal
1943, oil on canvas, 16×22 in.
Munson-Williams Proctor Institute Museum of Art,
Utica, NY

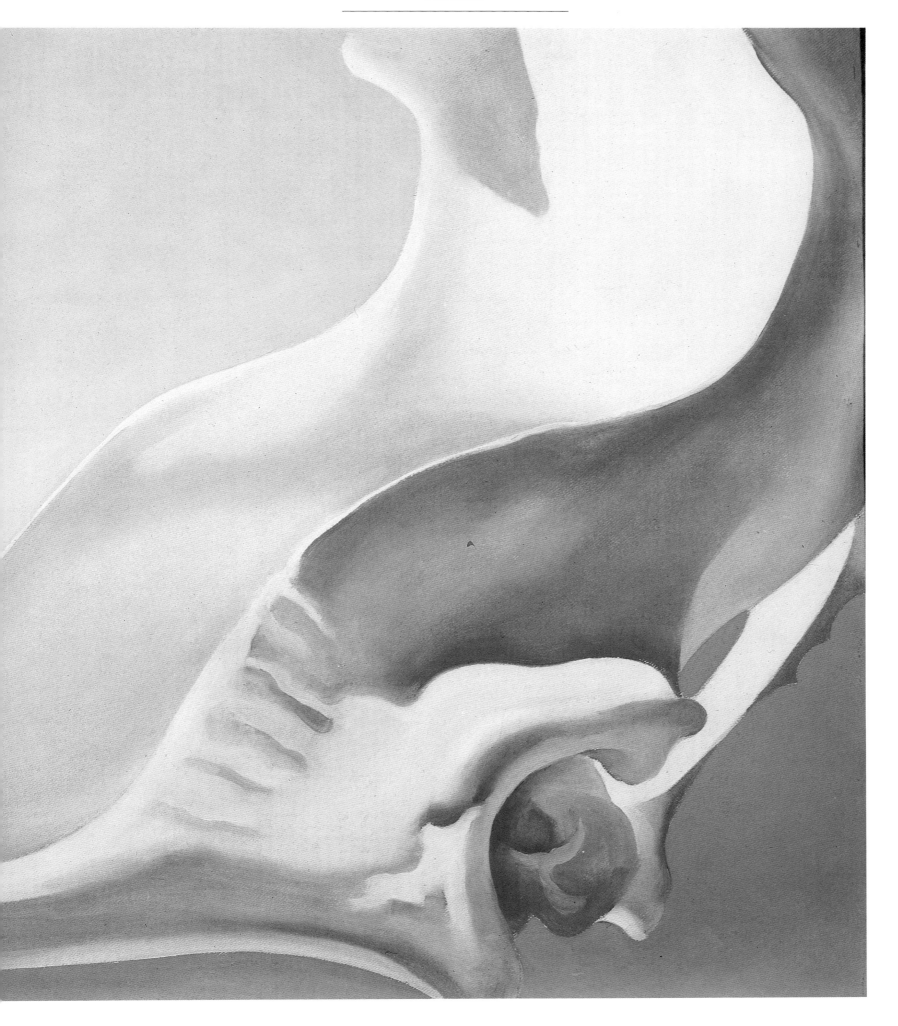

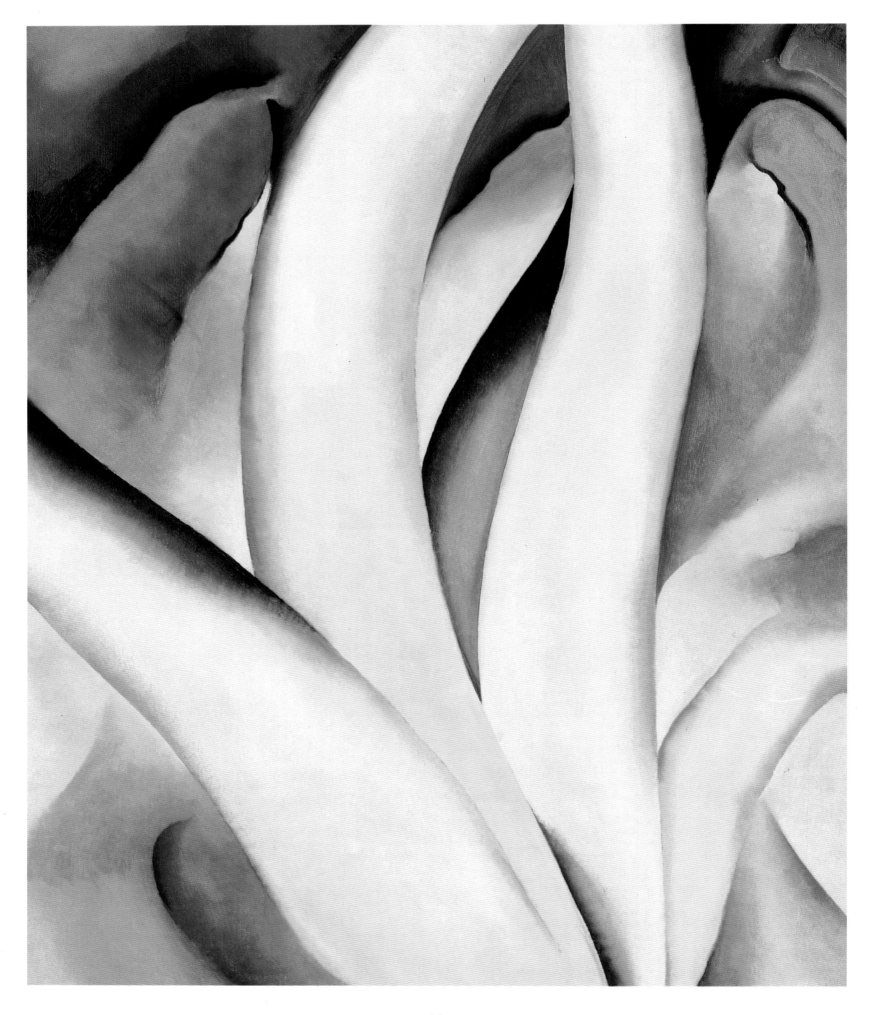

MINDSCAPES

The drawings that launched Georgia O'Keeffe toward the recognition she ultimately won were lines that thickened and slimmed, curved and curled with shadings of dark or light. Often she worked in series, investigating the thickness and thinness of a blue line, exploring a leaf, or a shell and shingle that she happened to look at together. They were abstractions yet they were based upon shapes she saw in nature and came directly from her emotional core. "It's as if my mind creates shapes that I don't know about. I get this shape in my head and sometimes I know where it comes from and sometimes I don't," she said some 60 years after Alfred Stieglitz first recognized her talent.

Even in her most representational works Georgia O'Keeffe was hardly a representational artist in the true sense of realism. But some of her abstractions we might call mindscapes to distinguish them from more recognizable objects, scenes, buildings or landscapes. Sometimes, as she herself said, she knew where they came from, and other times she did not.

She always loved music and became intrigued with the idea of translating it into something that the eye could see. She painted music in waves of pink layering over green and blue, as well as in blues and greens. As with her flowers, these passionate impressions are also frequently seen as erotically inspired.

"Try to paint your world as though you are the first man looking at it," she once advised someone. First she worked two lines in charcoal, then she tried several times to find their expression with black watercolor. Finally, she said, she got what she wanted with blue watercolor. O'Keeffe was able to invest a series of blue lines with her own individuality as surely as she was able to see a flower or the hills as no one else had seen them.

The *Evening Star* she painted in 1917 was in Canyon, Texas. That was where, as she described it, the wide, empty vistas surrounded one like an ocean. Even in daylight the evening star would already be high in the sky and it fascinated her. "My sister had a gun, and as we walked she would throw bottles into the air and shoot as many as she could before they hit the ground. I had nothing but to walk into nowhere and the wide sunset space with the star. Ten watercolors were made from that star," she later wrote.

Knowing the particular references and circumstances of a painting often enriches appreciation of the work. Sometimes the painting itself will spontaneously provoke a similar image from the viewer's memory. And sometimes no amount of puzzling will bring a viewer close to the artist's vision. *Wave, Night* rings true to the experience of being on a beach after dark. *Evening Star* may bear no resemblance to anything a Northeasterner will see at home, but perhaps it has an immediate familiarity to Texans of the plains. Many who travel by air will intuit a view from the airplane window in *It Was Blue and Green*.

It is inevitable that more philosophical impulses will be read into the works O'Keeffe did as she grew older. *Sky Above Clouds* is a huge work, the largest she ever did (8-by-24-feet). It illustrates her wonder at the scene she saw from an airplane window. It looks a lot like the Great Beyond itself, so to speak. This is her last major work, finished in 1965, when she was 78. It is as individual and unique as she was, and it carries a wonderful resonance with an earlier work, *Stars in a Dark Sky*, painted in 1917 at the age of 30: just 9-by-12-inches, is also a celestial scene, but of confetti-like, hard-edged stars rather than soft, fluffy white clouds.

It is appropriate to close with *Sky Above Clouds*, a work that shows how the artist's vision of the sky expanded. In both the early and the latest interpretation the sky is a reasonably well ordered place, stars or clouds lined up like members of a marching band. As she neared 80 her sky canvas became gargantuan, her effort heroic, monumental, the sky is light and infinite and the clouds float like stepping stones into a glowing pink sunset—it has the look of a benevolent hereafter.

Birch Trees at Dawn on Lake George
c. 1923, oil on canvas, 36×30 in.
Gift of Mrs. Ernest W. Stix,
The Saint Louis Art Museum, St. Louis, Missouri

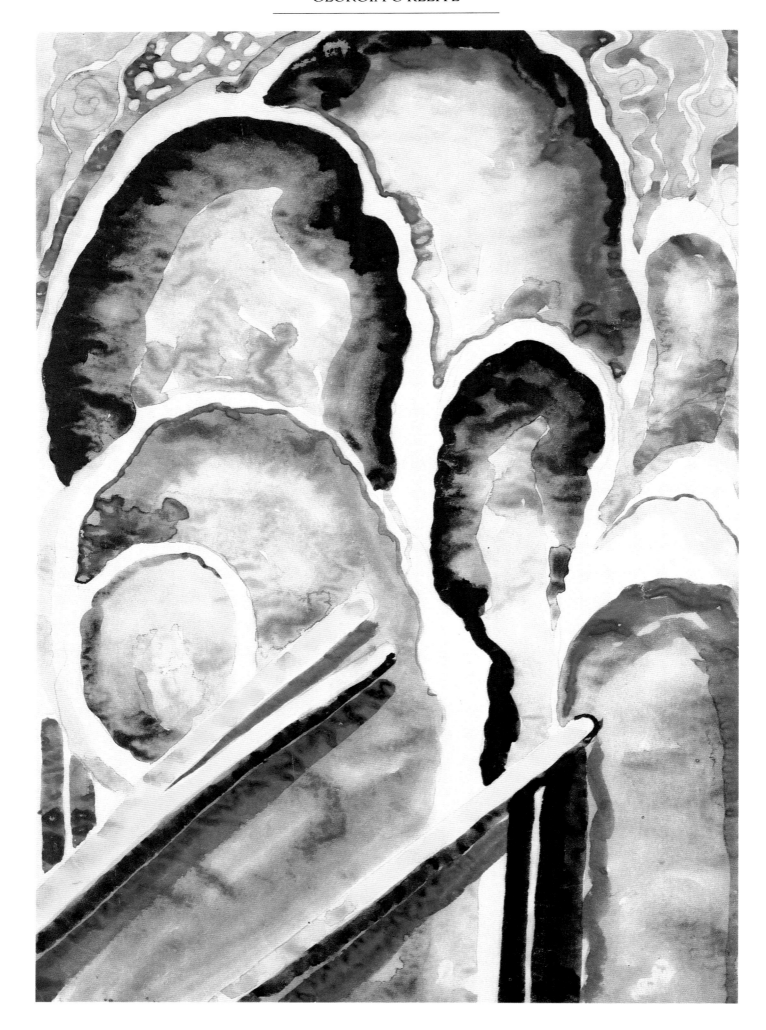

Blue #1
1916, watercolor on tissue paper, 16×11 in.
Bequest of Mary T. Crockcroft,
The Brooklyn Museum, Brooklyn, NY
(58.73)

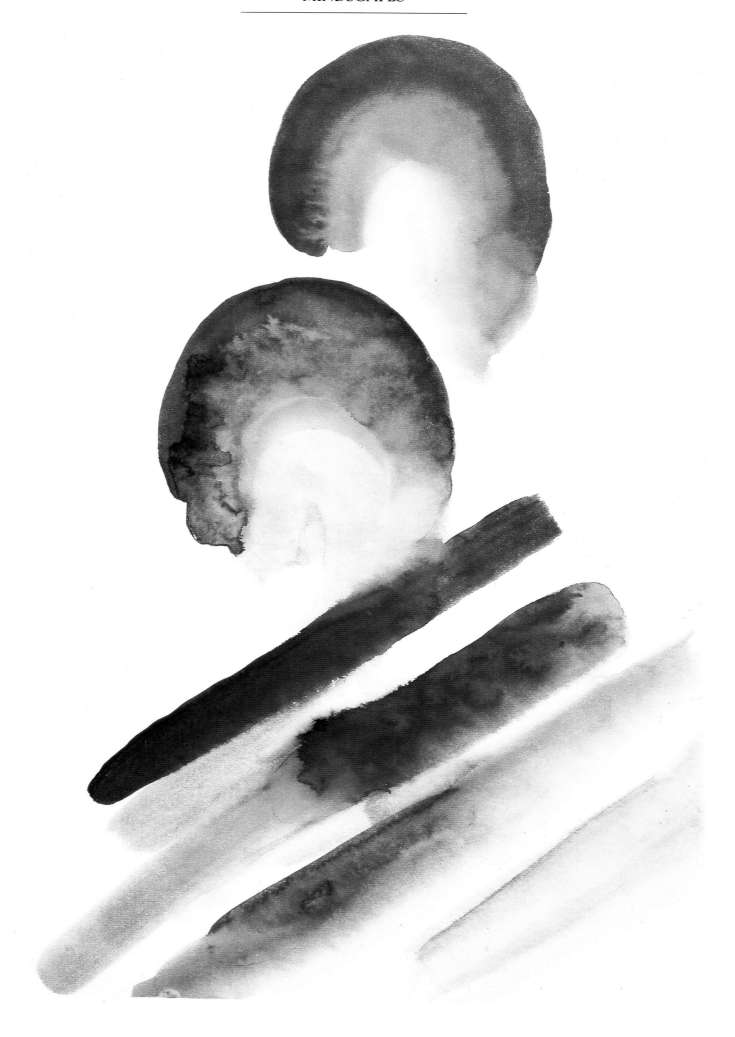

Blue #2,
1916, watercolor on tissue paper, 15⅞×10¹⁵⁄₁₆ in.
Bequest of Mary T. Crockcroft,
The Brooklyn Museum, Brooklyn, NY
(58.74)

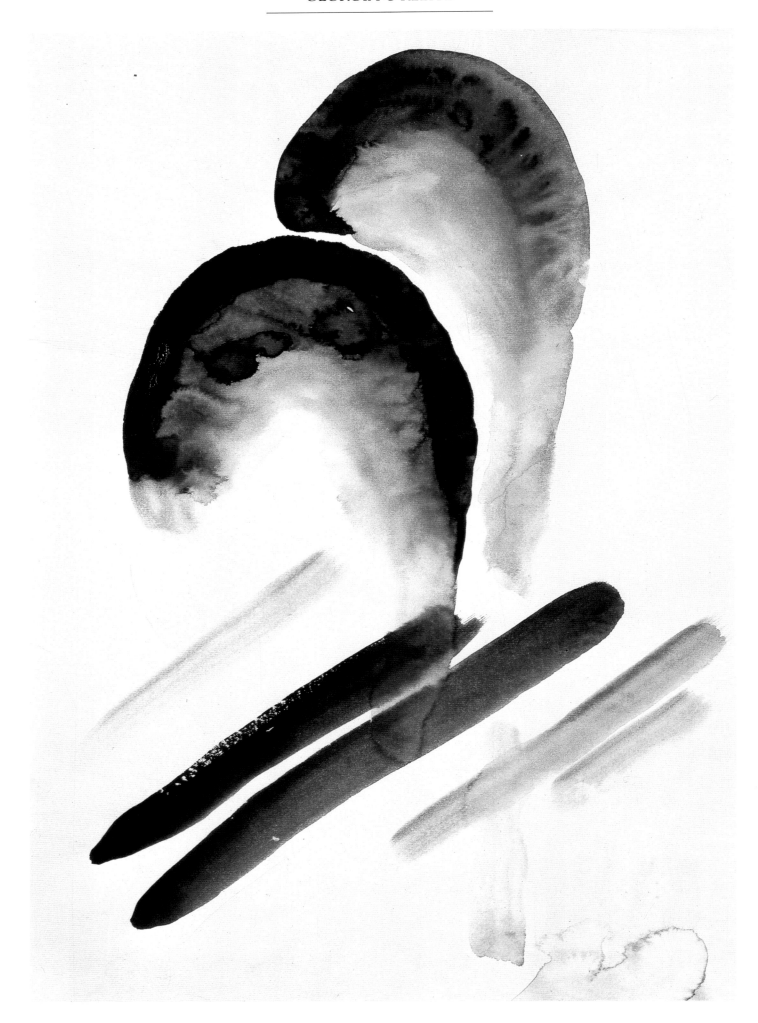

Blue #3
1916, watercolor on tissue paper, 15⅞×10¹⁵⁄₁₆ in.
Dick S. Ramsay Fund,
The Brooklyn Museum, Brooklyn, NY
(58.75)

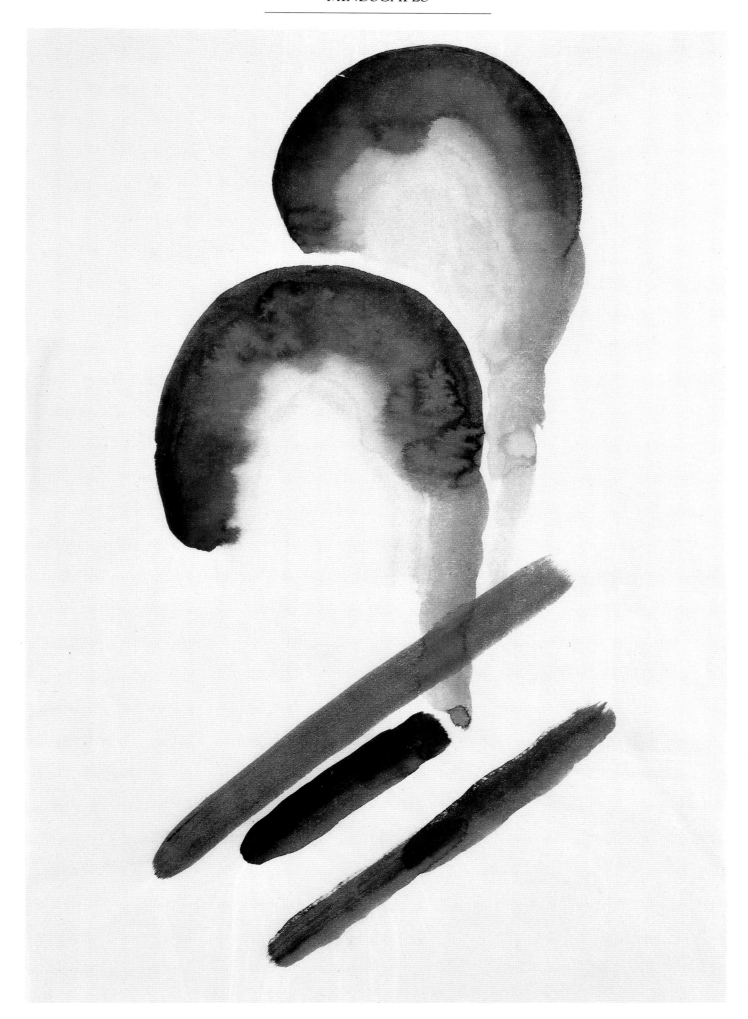

Blue #4
1916, watercolor on tissue paper, $15^{15}/_{16} \times 10^{15}/_{16}$ in.
Dick S. Ramsay Fund,
The Brooklyn Museum, Brooklyn, NY
(58.76)

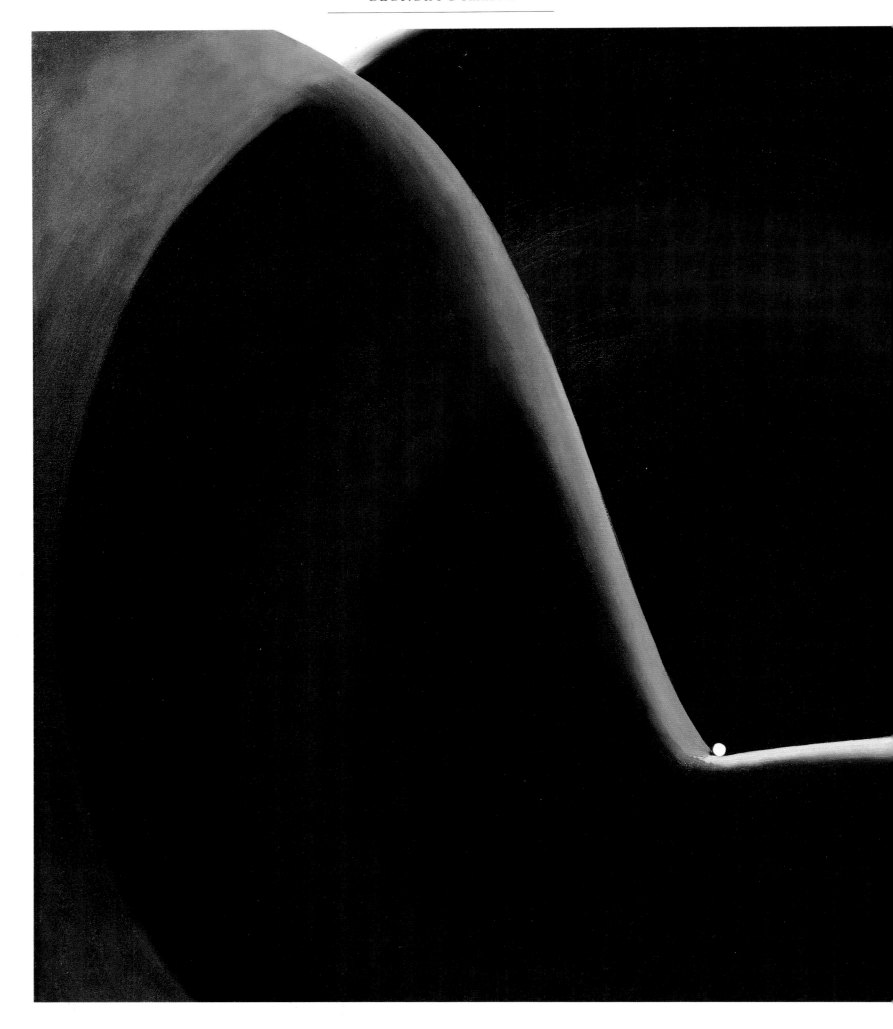

Black Abstraction
1927, oil on canvas, 30×40¼ in.
Alfred Stieglitz Collection,
The Metropolitan Museum of Art, New York, NY

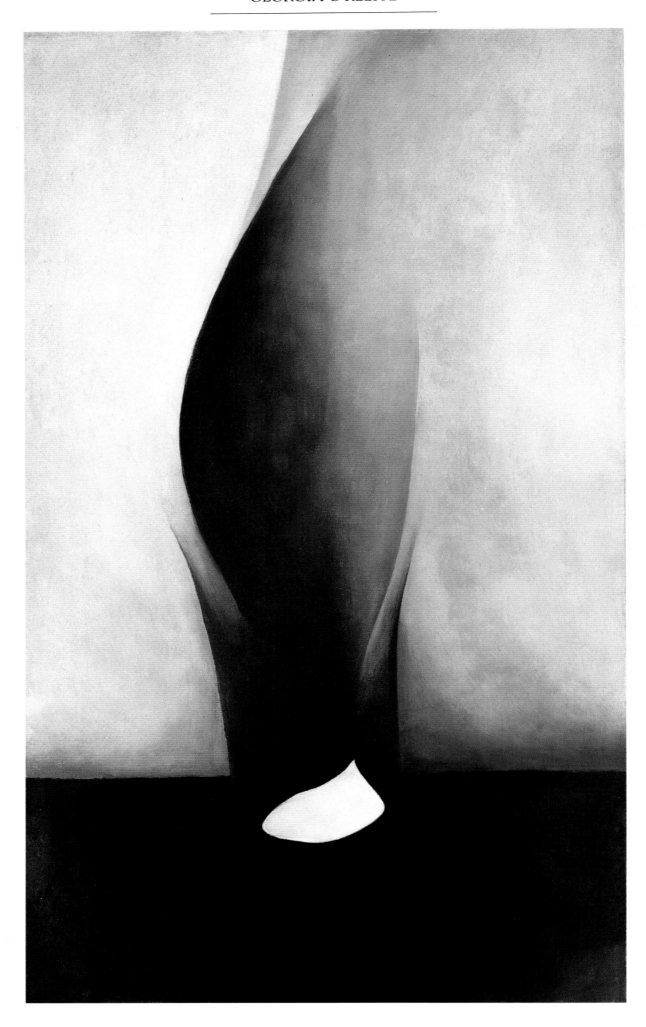

Shell and Shingle VI
1926, oil on canvas, 30¹⁄₁₆×17⅞ in.
Gift of Charles E. Claggett in memory of
Blanche Fischel Claggett,
The Saint Louis Art Museum, St. Louis, Missouri.

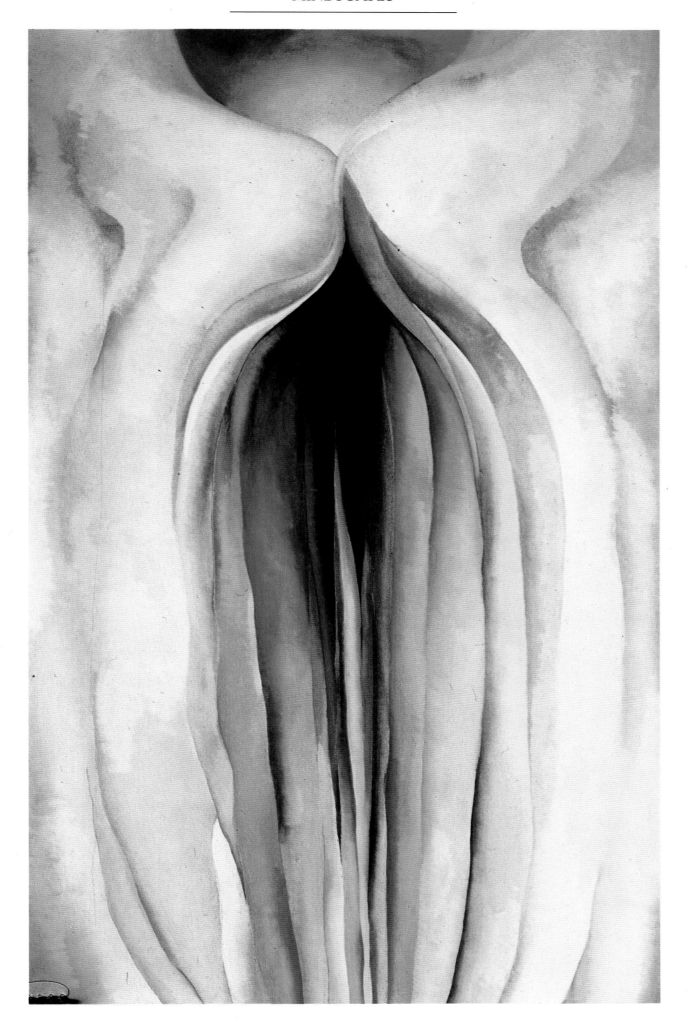

Grey Line with Black, Blue and Yellow
c. 1923, oil on canvas, 48×30 in.
Museum purchase with funds provided by the
Agnes Cullen Arnold Endowment Fund,
The Museum of Fine Arts, Houston, TX

Overleaf:
From the Plains I
1953, oil on canvas, 47¹¹⁄₁₆×83⅝ in.
Gift of the Estate of Tom Slick,
Marion Koogler McNay Art Institute,
San Antonio, TX

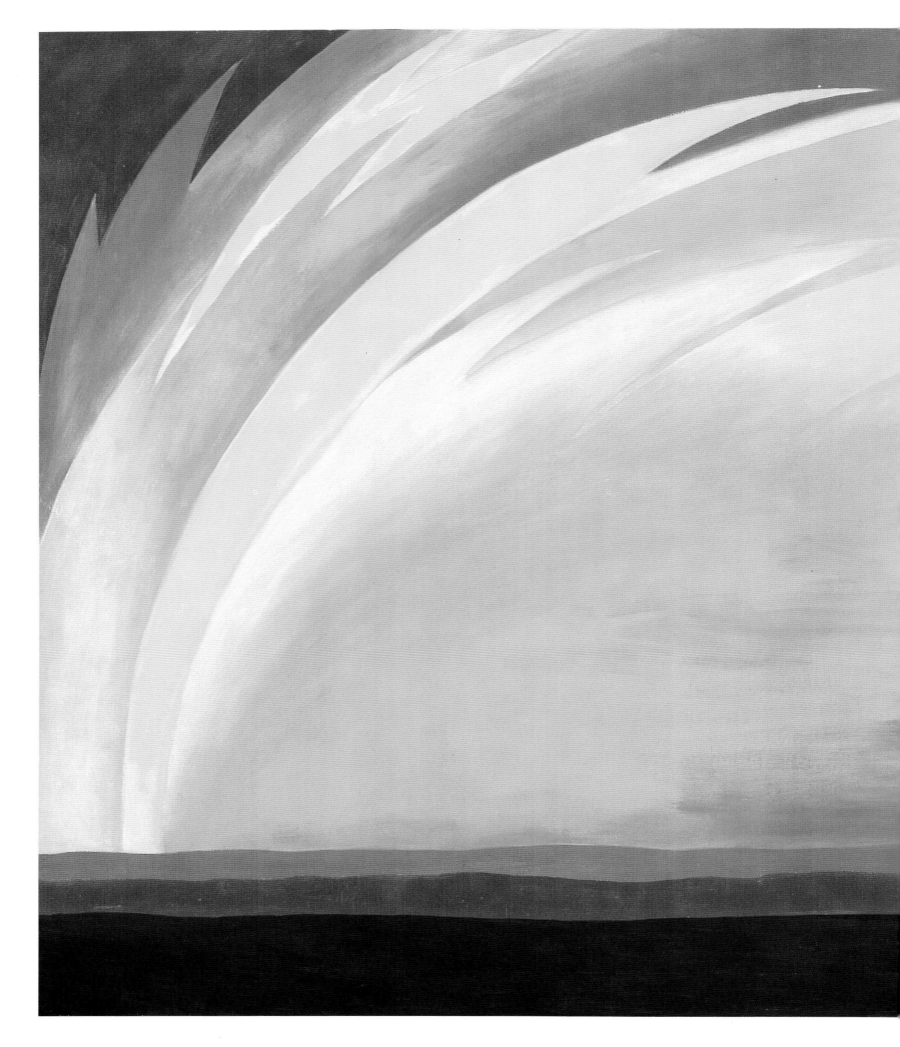

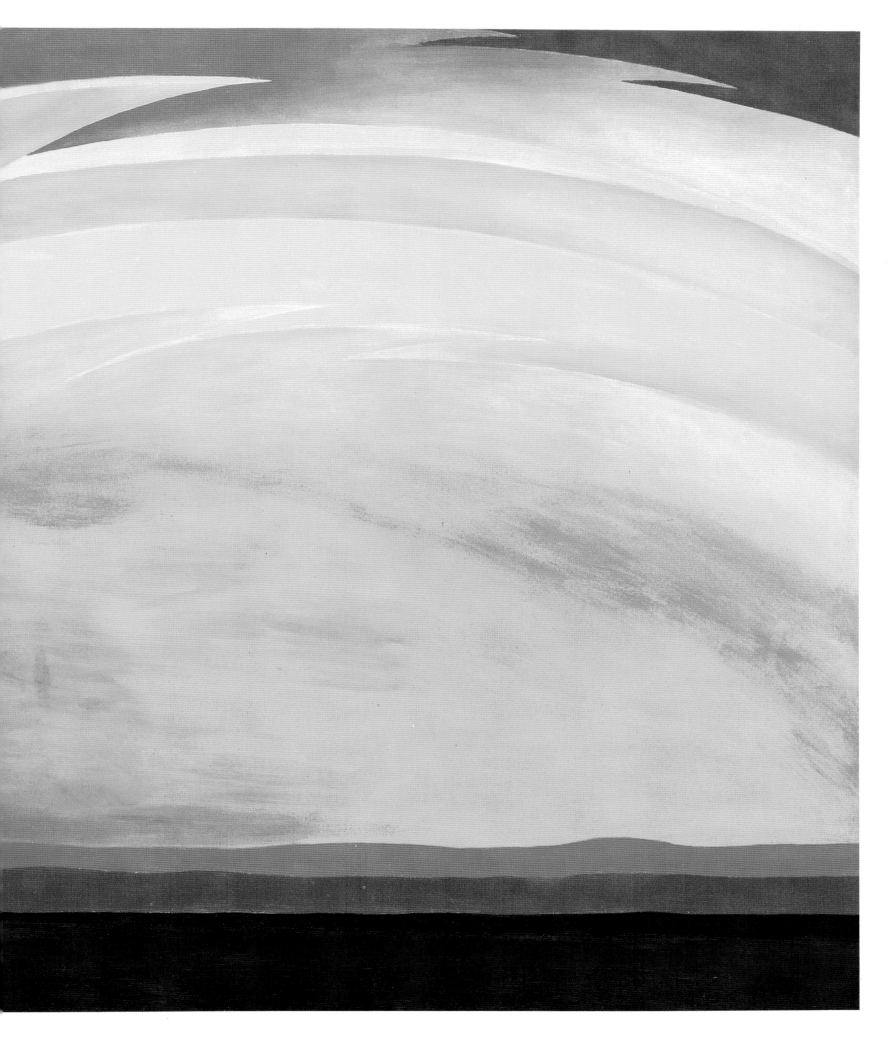

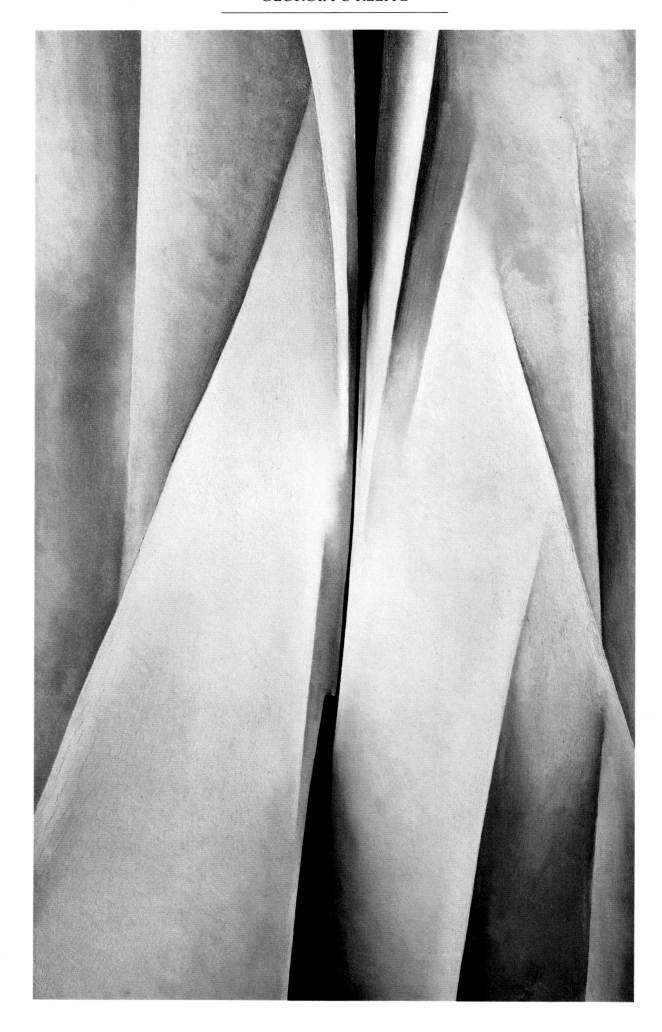

Abstraction
1926, oil on canvas, 30×18 in.
Purchased,
Collection of Whitney Museum of American Art,
New York, NY
(58.43)

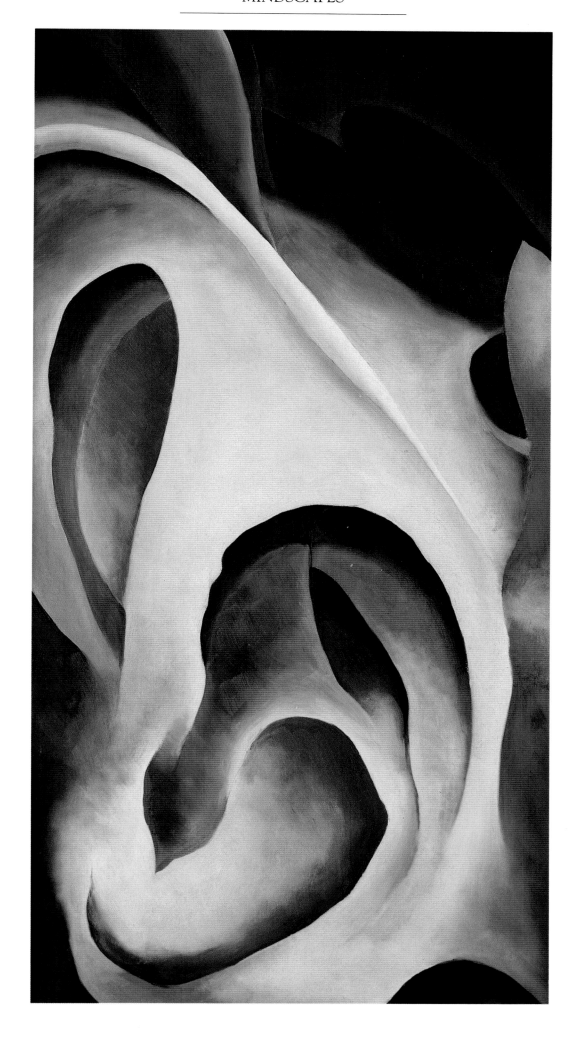

Leaf Motif #2
1924, oil on canvas, 35×18 in.
The Mary and Sylvan Lang Collection,
Marion Koogler McNay Art Institute,
San Antonio, TX

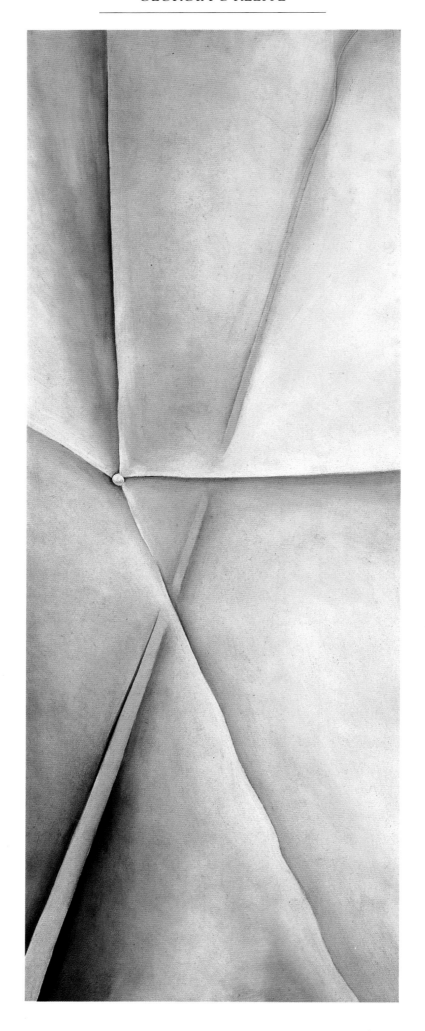

White Abstraction (Madison Avenue)
1926, oil on canvas, 32½×12 in.
Gift of Charles C. and Margaret Stevenson
Henderson in memory of Hunt Henderson,
Collection Museum of Fine Arts, St. Petersburg, FL

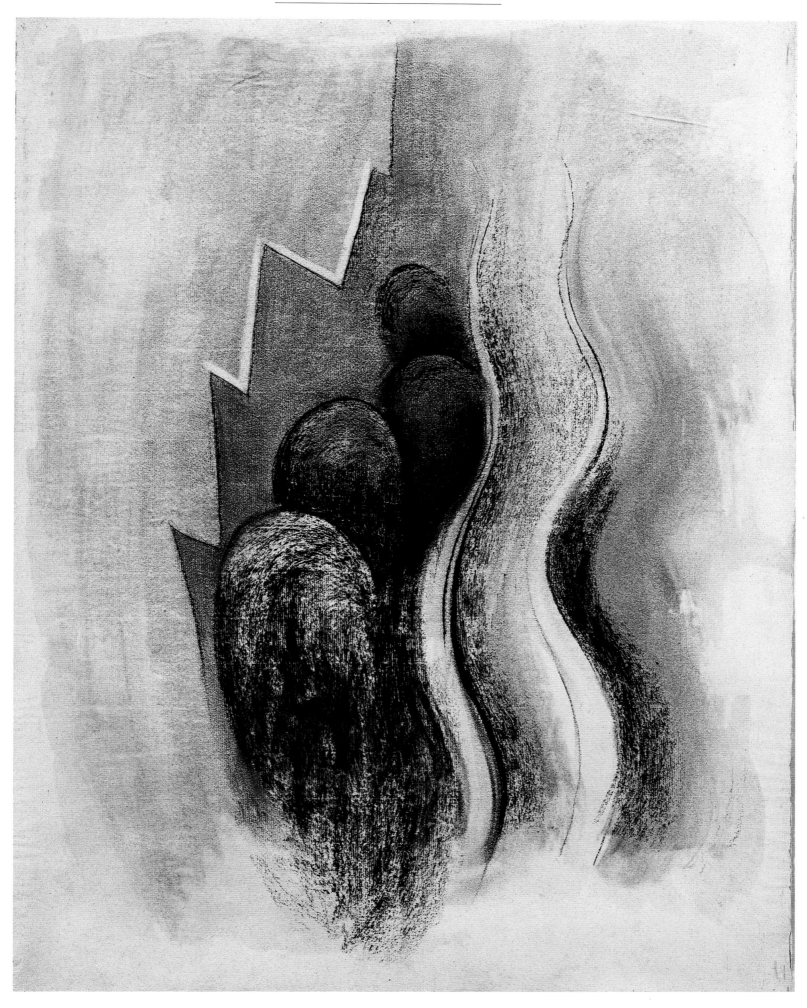

Drawing XIII
1915, Charcoal on paper, 24½×19 in.
The Alfred Stieglitz Collection, 1950,
The Metropolitan Museum of Art, New York, NY

Overleaf:
It Was Blue and Green
1960, oil on canvas, 30×40 in.
Lawrence H. Bloedel Bequest,
Collection of Whitney Museum of American Art,
New York, NY
(77.1.37)

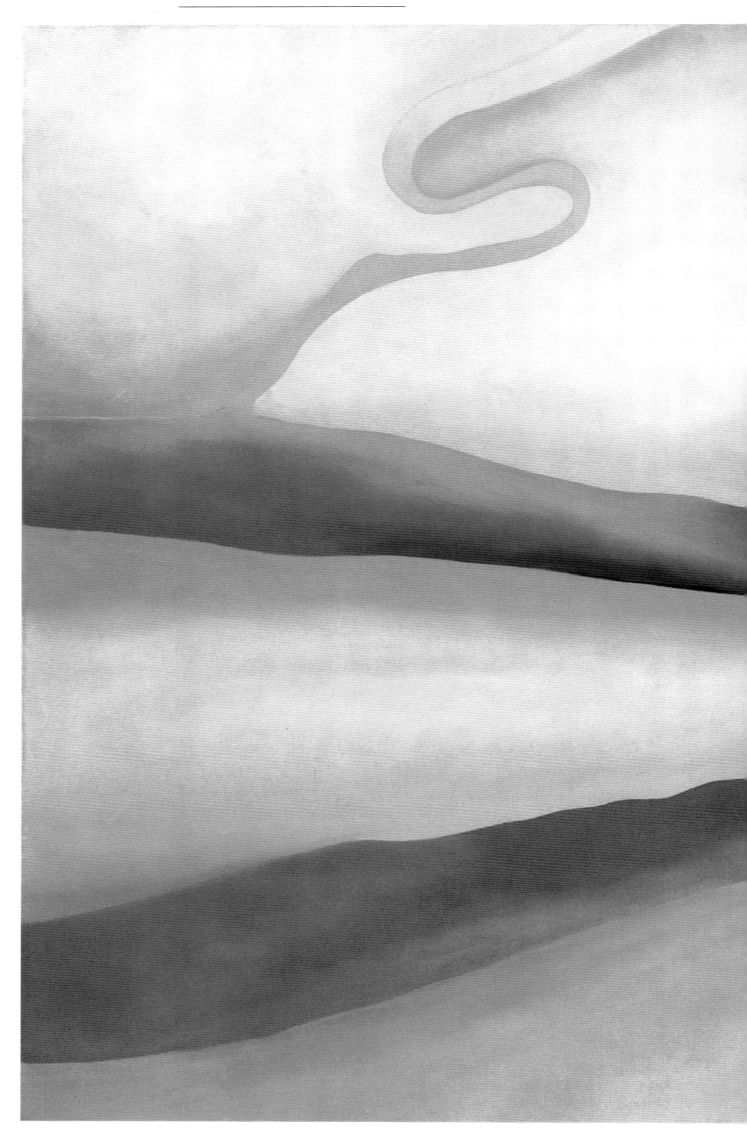

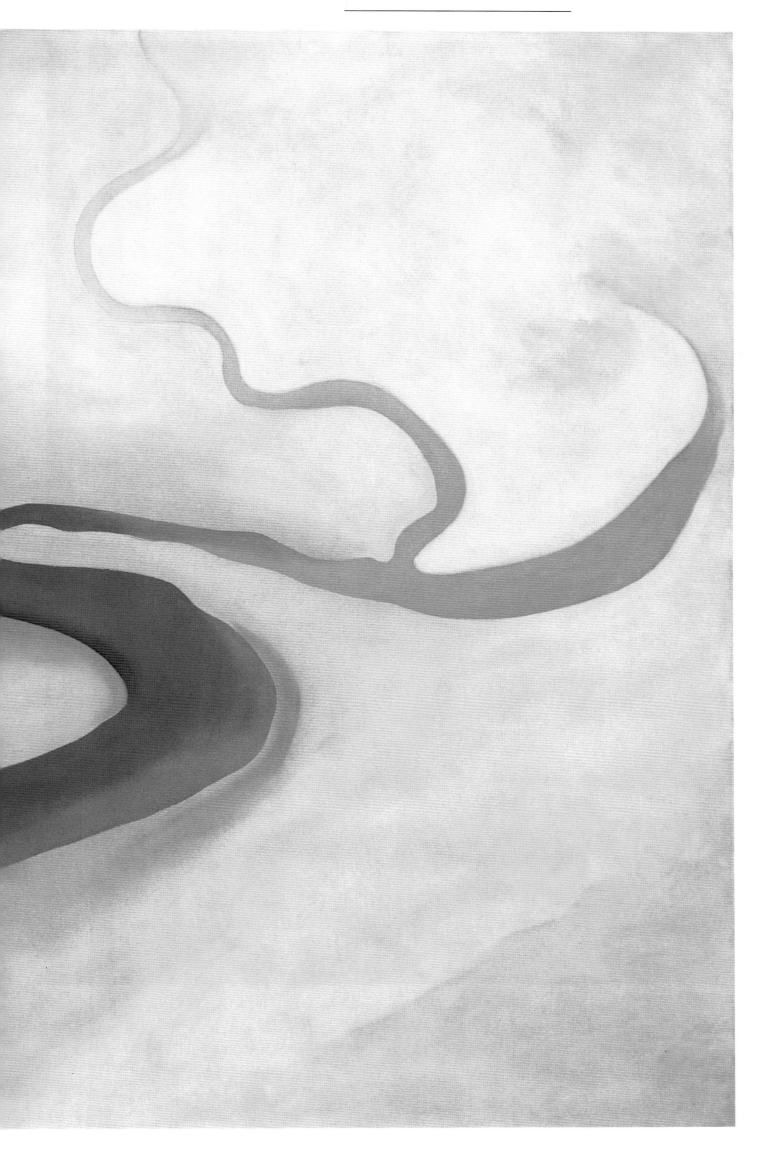

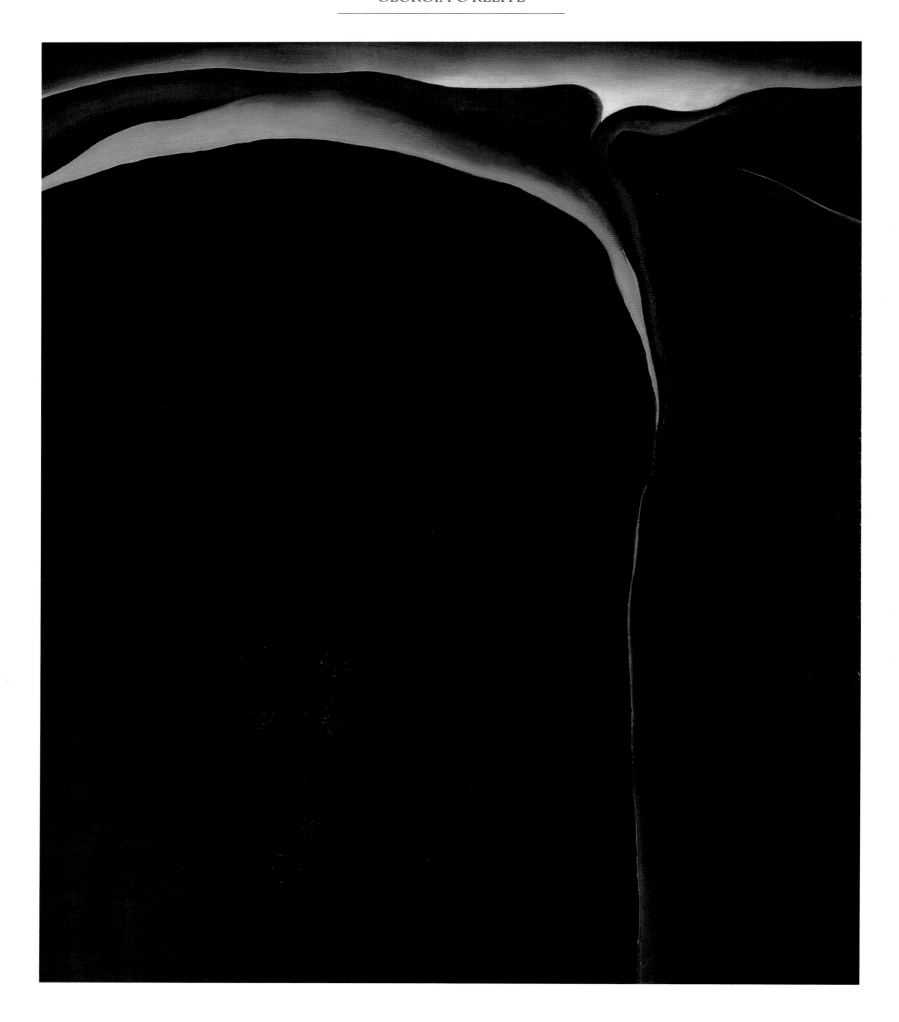

Dark Abstraction
1924, oil on canvas, 24⅞×20⅞ in.
Gift of Charles E. and Mary Merrill,
The Saint Louis Art Museum, St. Louis, Missouri

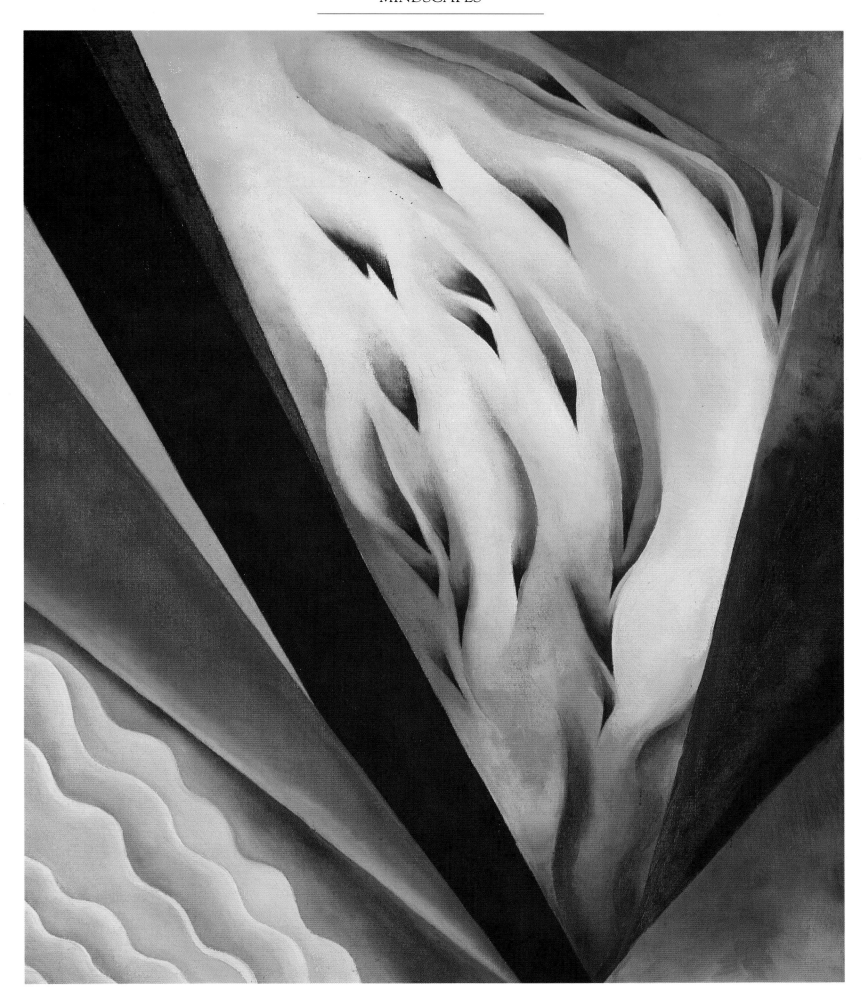

Blue and Green Music
1919, oil on canvas, 23×19 in.
Gift of Georgia O'Keeffe to the
Alfred Stieglitz Collection,
The Art Institute of Chicago, IL

Overleaf:
Evening Star No. V
1917, watercolor on paper, 8⅝×11⅝ in.
Bequest of Helen Miller Jones,
Marion Koogler McNay Art Museum,
San Antonio, TX
(1989.36)

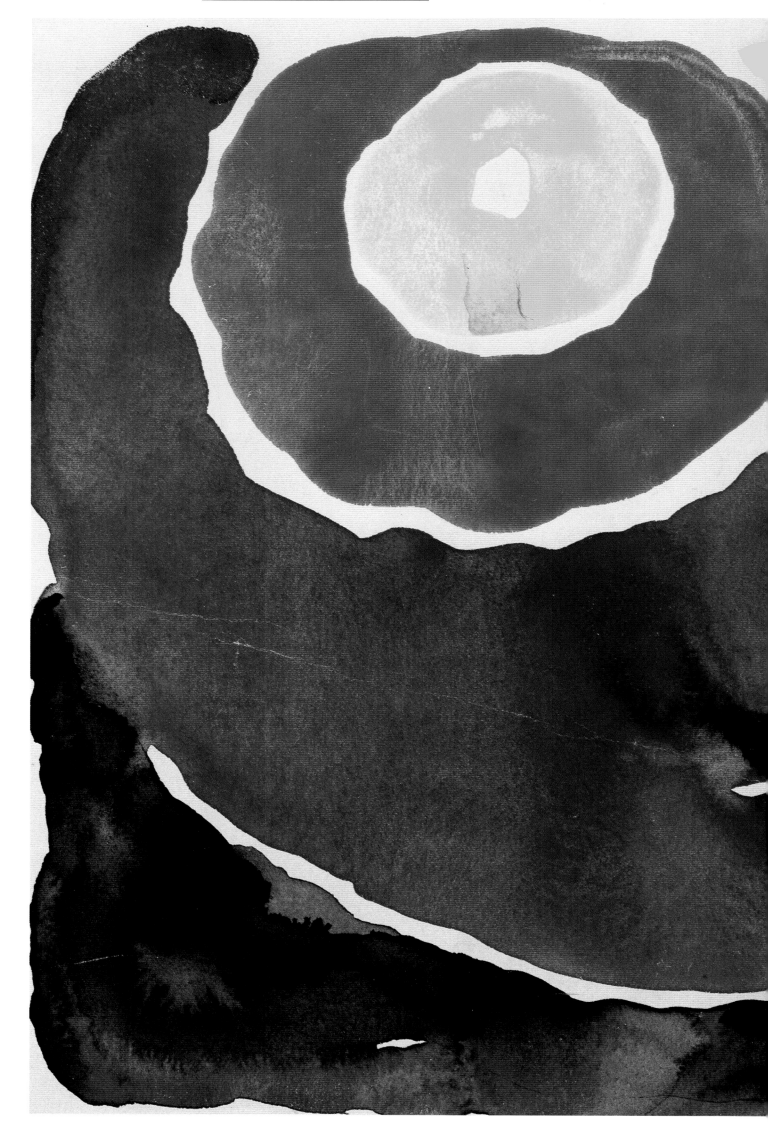

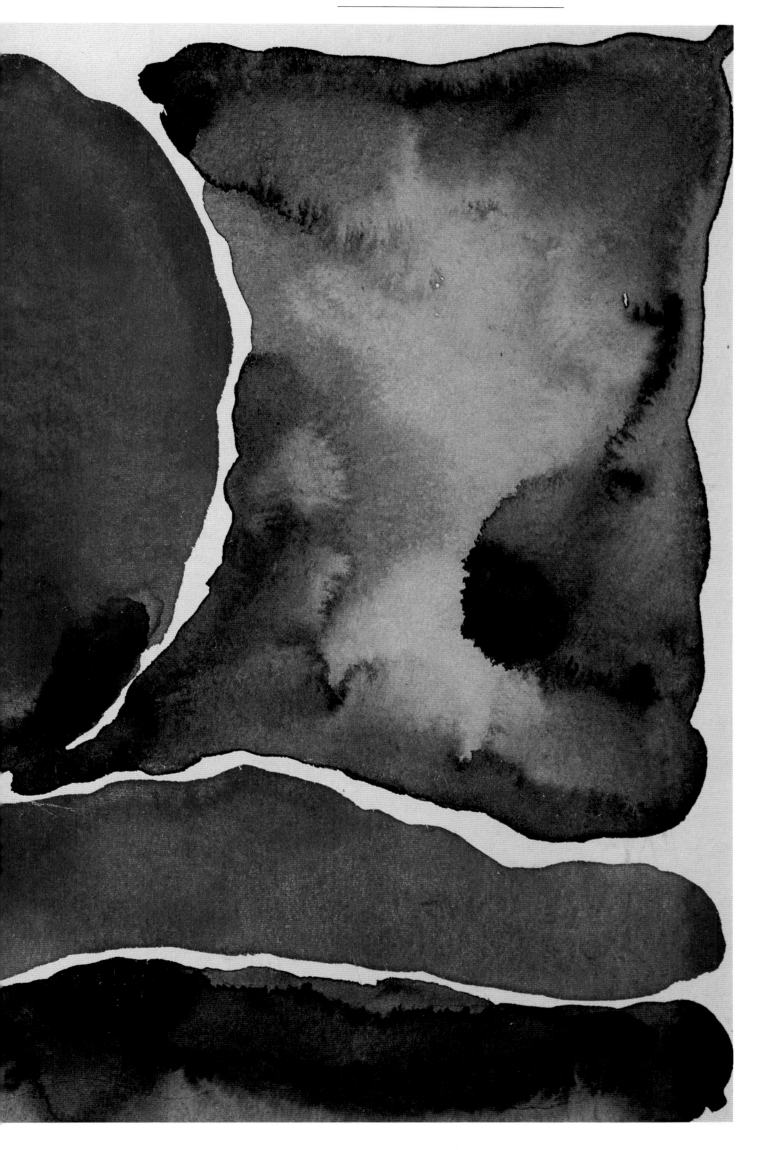

LIST OF COLOR PLATES

PHOTO CREDITS
All pictures were provided by the credited museum or gallery, except for those supplied by the following:
Archives of American Art, Smithsonian Institution, Washington, DC: 10.
Brompton Photo Library: 8-9.
UPI/Bettmann Newsphotos: 9, 12, 13, 15, 16-17, 18, 20, 21, 22, 23, 25.
ARTWORK
Page 6: Georgia O'Keeffe
Paul Strand, c. 1930
Photo, gelatin silver print, 7⅞×7⁷⁄₁₆ in.
National Portrait Gallery, Smithsonian Institution, Washington, DC
Page 7: Seated Nude X
Georgia O'Keeffe, 1917
Watercolor on paper, 11⅞×8⅞ in.
Van Day Truex Fund, 1981
The Metropolitan Museum of Art, NY, NY
Page 11: Nude Descending a Staircase
Marcel Duchamps, 1912
Oil on canvas, 58×35 in.
Louise and Walter Arensberg Collection,
Philadelphia Museum of Art, PA
© ADAGP, Paris, DACS, London, 1989

Pages 13-14: Shell and Feather
Georgia O'Keeffe, no date
Oil on canvas, 6×12 in.
Gift of Rowland Burdon-Muller
Colby College Art Museum, Waterville, ME
Page 19: The Figure 5 in Gold
Charles Demuth, 1928
Oil on composition board, 38×29¾ in.
The Alfred Stieglitz Collection
The Metropolitan Museum of Art, NY, NY
Page 24: Sky Above the Clouds IV
Georgia O'Keeffe, 1965
Oil on canvas, 95¾×287½ in.
Paul and Gabriella Rosenbaum Foundation Restricted Gift, and gift of Georgia O'Keeffe, © The Art Institute of Chicago, IL.
All Rights Reserved.